Investment Analysis for Income Properties

HONDROS
LEARNING™

HONDROS LEARNING™

4140 Executive Parkway

Westerville, Ohio 43081

www.hondroslearning.com

© 2016 by Hondros Learning™. All rights reserved

Published 2016. Printed in the United States of America

19 18 17 16   1 2 3 4

ISBN: 978-1-59844-270-0

For more information on or to purchase our products, please visit www.hondroslearning.com.

Table of Contents

PREFACE

Investment Analysis for Income Properties

Investment Analysis for Income Properties provides a thorough exploration of concepts, calculations, and processes involved in the analysis and valuation of income properties. The course delves into the steps of income property valuation and the foundation for the financial analysis of income properties. The various types of gross income (and their influence), gross income streams, as well as the conversion of income into a value indicator via multiplier capitalization is reviewed. Development of the NOI is reviewed and the course presents a presentation of how income production's performance, durability, and quality is found through performance ratios. The calculation to find the capitalization rate for direct capitalization is presented and examined. The course concludes with an introductory level exploration of how compound interest is processed and applied to the Income Approach.

Course Learning Objectives

- Identify the appraisal process, investor concepts, and real estate agent duties.
- Describe how Income Production Economic Principles are divided into the categories of Productivity and Marketability.
- Define the appraisal process and the development process of finding a Net Operating Income Statement.
- Contrast the difference between contract rent and market rent.
- Define how to analyze market rent and how to make adjustments for that analysis.
- Describe how to properly compose a market rent schedule.
- Define the roles of vacancy and credit loss and other income in the development of Effective Gross Income.
- Identify how to process Gross Market Rent, Potential Gross Income, and Effective Gross Income and how to perform multiplier capitalization.
- Describe the process of extracting and concluding market rent.
- Define risk evaluation components.
- Identify how to develop four types of multipliers and the process of formulating the estimate of a future dollar amount needed.
- Identify how to calculate the annual payment future worth at a compounded rate of interest.
- Describe how to differentiate between fixed and variable operating expenses.
- Identify a reserve estimate for the replacement of short-lived items.
- Describe how to forecast cost and depreciation.
- Identify how many parking spaces should be allotted for proposed or available units.
- Define the process for concluding gross monthly rent.
- Describe how to calculate necessary equity when debt leveraging is the goal.
- Describe how to extract a capitalizations rate through the market method and the role of debt leveraging in the development of a cap rate.
- Identify how to conclude a value using the IRV method.
- Describe how to forecast future cost based on a compounded rate and describe the impact of time on money.
- Identify which compound interest column is applicable in developing an Income Approach.

Hondros Learning

Hondros Learning™ is a leading provider of classroom materials for mortgage pre-licensing and continuing education. Together with Hondros College, we have provided training and educational products for more than one million students. For more information about CompuCram test preparation products or any of our other products, please visit www.hondroslearning.com and, www.compucram.com.

Acknowledgments

Hondros Learning™ thanks the following experts for their valuable contributions and assistance in developing this text:

Timothy Detty
Certified General Appraiser
AQB-Certified USPAP Instructor

Diana T. Jacob
Certified General Appraiser
AQB-Certified USPAP Instructor
Real Estate Instructor

Chapter 1:
The Three Perspectives of Value

Chapter Objectives

After completing this chapter, you will be able to:

- Identify the appraisal process, investor concepts, and real estate agent duties.
- Describe how income production economic principles are divided into the categories of Productivity and Marketability.
- Define the appraisal process.
- Describe the development process of finding a Net Operating Income Statement.

Appraisal Process A sequential series of steps in critical reasoning that produces a defined value.

Economic Principles Governing truisms in the appraisal process that identify motivations and decisions.

Net Operating Income Cash remaining after rental income is processed for market conditions and expenditures with operating the income property.

Key Terms

Chapter Introduction

The valuation of income property types begins with basic economic concepts that define the actions of the market participants. The investor, the agent, and the appraiser view property value from different perspectives. This chapter introduces economic principles that relate specifically to the Income Approach and gives an introductory summary of the appraisal process and Net Operating Income Statements. These two sequenced processes, in conjunction with the economic principles, serve as the foundation for the financial analysis of income property.

All purchases and leases of property are investments of some sort. Whether living in a tenant-occupied property or currently owning a property, real property owners can enjoy financial benefits. The measure of benefit in some property types is the production of income. The income production is part of both *freehold* (owner's position) and *non-freehold* (tenant position) interest. Most investors and licensed real estate agents will see this benefit as holding an interest in real estate. Technically speaking **real property interest** is *the position of rights and privileges to the real estate*, real estate being the land as improved. In 49 of the 50 states, *ownership with the full "bundle of rights and privileges"* is known as a **freehold interest**, (the fee simple interest unencumbered). In Louisiana, the outlier, that interest, which essentially has the same legal benefit, is known as the "Full Complete and Perfect" interest with a "Triangle of Rights" (**Abusus,** *the right to mortgage, or the right to give away,* **Fructus***, the rights to the fruits or income benefits,* and **Usus,** *the right to occupy, lease, enter and exit*). In Louisiana, under the Napoleonic Code, the law has no allowance for interpretation; it requires the letter of law application. In the common law of the remaining 49 states, court precedents and interpretations of past cases are used to resolve conflicts in ownerships and rights to use.

A tenant position is a non-freehold interest and by virtue of the leased tenant position, the tenant holds the "leasehold interest." The owner holds an encumbered fee interest known as the "leased fee interest." Think of it this way, *If I have the right to lease part of my ownership in fee, I have a leased-fee interest. If I hold a lease, I have the leasehold interest, the right to enter and exit at will to use, (within the bounds of the lease covenants), and in some cases, the right to sublease.* Both positions have value.

Valuation Perspectives of Interest in Real Property

The value of income-producing property is viewed from distinctly different positions that represent market participants and related interested parties. State-licensed agents who represent the interested parties have a completely different purview and statutory obligations than the valuation expert, known as the real property appraiser. Both licensed agents and state-certified/licensed appraisers will view the property, and both will form an opinion about the marketability and the value. Often, the agent will call the value, "market price," while the appraiser will conclude what is known as a "market value."

The investor (sometimes called the consumer) may be the seller, the buyer, or even the tenant. From their individual perspective, income-producing property types will have a characteristic that will appeal to their individual demands. As a seller, the investor will often have a need to either sell or possibly consider refinancing a property. In both instances, the seller will focus on the maximum net of the sale or maximum mortgage value that can be obtained (in the case of a refinance). As a buyer, the perspective will seek the best (often lowest) price that can be agreed upon in order to purchase the property, whether to be for owner-occupancy or for an investment in rental property. What few buyers realize is that a licensed agent, by law, must work toward meeting the needs of the individual who is paying the commission for the sale. In most instances, that means helping the seller reach the highest possible price when negotiating a sale or when executing a lease (in which case the highest net rent is the goal).

Economic Principles of the Income Approach

Economic principles must exist to support the process of evaluation for any analysis of property. This includes:

- Real property
- Personal property
- Intangible property of business valuation

When the focus of the valuation has a greater emphasis on the income, there are governing economic principles that must be kept in mind. Economic principles can be separated into **two (2) divisions** and **three (3) categories**.

Two Divisions of Economic Principles

There are two (2) divisions of economic principles. These divisions include the:

- **Principles of Productivity**
- **Principles of Marketability**

Principles of Productivity

The Principles of Productivity include:

- Surplus Productivity
- Balance
- Contribution
- Increasing and Decreasing Returns
- Highest and Best Use
- Anticipation
- Opportunity Costs
- Agents of Production
- Marginal Utility

Principles of Marketability

The Principles of Marketability include:

- Supply and Demand
- Change
- Externalities
- Competition
- Integration, Equilibrium, Decline, and Renewal
- Conformity
- Substitution

Three Categories of Economic Principles

The three (3) categories of economic principles include:

- **Land and Improvement Principles**
- **User Principles**
- **Market Area Principles**

Land and Improvement Principles

The land and improvement principles include:

- Balance
- Surplus Productivity
- Contribution
- Agents of Production
- Highest and Best Use

Land and Improvement Principle Highlights

The principles included in the land and improvement principle category are summarized to provide a further exploration of how they relate to the Income Approach.

Agents of Production

There are **four** (4) agents of production (sometimes known as elements) that are directly connected to the principle of balance and the principle of surplus productivity. The four (4) agents of production are:

1. Labor
2. Capital
3. Coordination
4. Land

> √ **Note:** Land is **always** the last agent to be satisfied. Value is maximized when these agents are in proper proportion (according to the market).

When gathering information, individuals with different roles will highlight specific points of information about an income property.

- **Investors:** The investor will not want to invest in any property where income cannot be maximized by the agents of production. If proposed construction is involved, the investor will look carefully at how the land can be utilized to maximize the income production.

- **Licensed Agents:** The licensed agent will research other properties in the market to include rental information to supply the investor with comparable data allowing them to make reasonable offers that will optimize the investor's decision to purchase. What will generally be lacking is the understanding of *what the investor will want to yield*.

- **Appraisers:** The appraiser, when gathering information about income property, will look at the type of income property (e.g., one-to-four unit apartments, detached single-family, etc.) and then the absorption rate of the gross leasable space, along with reasonable expectations of vacancy and credit loss. A study of other similar properties will be analyzed, not only for the price that was paid, but also for the expected **equity dividend rate** and **equity yield rate** so that a strong financial analysis can be presented to assist the investor in making a knowledgeable decision about buying or selling.

Balance

This principle interplays with the principle of supply and demand, which is one of the Principles of Marketability. Since the principle of balance is the **competitive** positioning of the subject's site as improved, it is specific to its productivity from the site's location.

The **principle of balance** is *an economic display of the buyer's preference for on-site amenities as they relate to a property's function.* Value is, in theory, maximized when the four agents of production are in proper balance. Balance in this context as defined doesn't mean equal proportion; it means that the components or elements in their state of interaction are in a state of equilibrium.

1. **Labor** represents *the manpower necessary to develop the property.*
2. **Capital** represents *the money necessary to fund the development.*
3. **Coordination/Entrepreneurship** represents *the profit to the developer/investor.*
4. **Land** represents *the real estate component.*

Land is always the last agent to be satisfied even though often it is the first component of acquisition. The reason this is that when the total investment is analyzed and broken down, the target yield of the investment is impacted when *any* of the components coming together are not in proper proportion.

Before a positive yield can be recognized, all elements must be accounted for or the investor will risk a negative yield in the investment. The **yield**, *the return on the investment,* may be positive or negative until the return of the land, capital cost, and labor have been satisfied. This concept also plays a part in the land ratio to the overall property value.

Example

The project has been selected and income potential has been analyzed. The investor has established the cost of the materials, understands financing costs, and has identified the cost of the labor needed to develop the land with a desire to earn a return on the investment of **25%**. The range of yield for a few similar small professional office property types has reached the high end of 25%, but most investors of similar income properties are realizing a yield of 18% to 22%, which appears to be most realistic. The investor sets out to purchase the land with the target yield of 25%.

- Market research results are a predominant range of 18%-22% yield on small professional offices.
- The investor's goal is a 25% yield.

Considering all factors, the investor knows the maximum he can spend for land is **$50,000**, if the 25% yield is to be realized. Real estate agents in the market area have identified available lots that can be purchased, but the list prices are from $65,000 to $70,000. An appraiser is engaged to appraise one of the lots available for purchase, and confirms the low end of the adjusted sales range for the land is $55,000, but it could be worth as much as $65,000 on the high end. The investor submits an offer for the land at $49,000, to which the seller counters at $60,000. The seller makes it known that the least amount that will be accepted is $55,000.

- In order to yield 25%, the maximum cost to acquire the land is $50,000.
- Available lots in the area are priced from $65,000 to $70,000.
- An appraisal confirms the low end of the adjusted range is $55,000, with the high end as much as $65,000.
- A counteroffer by the seller firmly held to $55,000; if the investor accepts, the yield would be considered disproportionate as the acquisition of the land cost was greater than necessary to achieve a 25% yield.

At this point, the investor must go back to the drawing board and make the decision: Is the desire to improve the site worth the effort, time, and risk for a lower yield? If the answer is yes, then the investment return will occur, but it will occur with a *disproportionate yield*, as the land cost went beyond the proportionate share or land ratio needed to achieve the 25% desired return.

√ **Caution!:** It's important not to confuse *balance* with *equal proportion*. Proper balance is a function of the market from a production standpoint on land and improvements. In some locations, the land will possess a greater share of the value. In other locations, the demand is so high that, in spite of the land, capital, and coordination costs, the yield will be higher due to that *escalated demand*.

For example, if the one-to-four unit property was built on a lot held as a speculative land investment for a period, and now there is a redistricting of a preferred school zone that encompasses that location, the land cost is low, having been previously acquired. The cost to construct may not have escalated, as the location is easily accessed and a staff of construction crews may be readily available if the contractor is sizeable enough to shuffle crews to the site from another project. At that point, investors will gladly pay a price for income-producing property that will offer them a positive cash flow, because they can command a higher rent per unit. It's a win-win for the builder/investor and the buyer/investor.

Contribution

The **principle of contribution** is *the economic driver that determines the worth or the amount of the dollar adjustments used in the Sales Comparison Approach.* It represents identified decisions of buyers who, if not allowed to buy the subject, would view a comparable transaction through an adjustment process. The extraction of the market reaction to differences in the comparable properties can be based on:

- **Paired sales analysis**
- **Regression analysis**
- Other factors such as **interviews** or through **identifying percentage reactions** (in a qualified judgment)

There must be support for the adjustment, which is made to stabilize the price (adjusting the price for differences between the sale known as a comparable and the subject). It cannot be an unsupported conclusion.

Highest and Best Use

Highest and best use is *an economic land principle that is also part of the appraisal process in a market value opinion.* Highest and best use drives the selection of comparable transactions (sales and rentals) in the development of the market value opinion. It is a conclusion after tests are applied that results in the land being maximally productive. Whereas the market value represents a most probable price, it is a probable price that can be *obtained when a land and its improvements are being the "best they can be."*

The existing use that is the current use may be *different* from a property's highest and best use. Existing use is a decision of the owner; highest and best use is a decision of the market.

Surplus Productivity

The principle of surplus productivity speaks to the concept of the remainder of net income. *The net income remaining after the agents of production have been satisfied* is known as **surplus productivity**. Any additional funds that remain are generally attributable to the land.

Remember, the four agents of production are:

1. Labor
2. Capital
3. Coordination
4. Land

These agents are integral to this economic principle and the principle of balance (when in proper proportion, the balance value is maximized). When an excess occurs, after all agents have been satisfied, the surplus or residual income is attributed to the land.

Understanding these economic principles will enable better understanding of the role they play in the financial analysis of residential income property types. The value of a property is dependent on *the perspective of the individual or entity judging the value*. Regardless of whether it's the investor, the tax assessor, the agent or the tenant, all will have a perspective of the "cash in exchange" through a logical process that has its focus on the needs. For the appraiser, part of solving the problem for value comes through a sequential, logical reasoning that is known as the appraisal process.

User Principles

The user principles include:

- Anticipation
- Substitution
- Opportunity Costs
- Increasing and Decreasing Returns

User Principle Highlights

All principles included in the user principle category are highlighted and summarized to provide a further exploration of how they relate to the Income Approach.

Anticipation

The present value of a property is a current worth by the expectation of a future benefit. The price paid for real estate represents *the investor's opinion of the current value that includes the investor's forecast of benefits*. The price paid is a *representation* of that present worth. It is a discounted price based on an anticipated use and expected resale of the asset. To yield both a financial return on and of the investment, the price paid for the property should consider the risk the investor has taken with this equitable investment.

Under the principle of anticipation, the price paid is a discounted value of the future price. The premise of that concept in a current price being a discounted value is rooted in the assumption of the right to receive one dollar in the future. If the expectation is that a dollar will be received (anticipated) in the future then it cannot be worth one dollar today; it is likely worth less than one dollar.

When working with the principle of anticipation, licensed agents and appraisers have different roles.

- **Licensed Agent Role**: The role of the agent is to assist in the negotiation of the offer to purchase. When it is a buyer representation, the agent will focus on the future needs of the investor, working hard *to make the offer attractive to the seller or seller agent*. Part of what may be involved is the number of days on the market (DOM) the property has been listed. Seeking a property that meets the investor's need for a target yield will often direct the licensed agent into a search for listings near their expiration date. It is a sign of potential softening on behalf of the seller, if the need to sell becomes more pressing as time passes.

- **Appraiser Role:** For the appraiser, a study of sales with focus on the reason for the purchase and the income projections, along with a study of the **equity dividend rates** (*annual dollars of profit after debt service measured against the equity invested*) will be necessary. That focus will give the investor a better understanding of the asset they have chosen to invest and the anticipated benefit based on the historical performance.

Substitution

In the Sales Comparison Approach the conclusion of market value is derived from the methodology of viewing sales with similar characteristics based on the market participant's judgment to pay no more for a property than a reasonable substituting property can be obtained.

Of the three approaches to value, the Sales Comparison Approach derives a value indication based on adjusted sale prices from transactions of similar properties purchased for similar investment purposes. For income-producing properties, the comparative concept flows into the comparison of:

- Market rents
- Capitalization rates
- Equity yield and dividend rates
- Multipliers, etc.

Increasing and Decreasing Returns

This principle of increasing and decreasing returns integrates with the components of the principle of balance's four agents of production. Because land cannot be moved, nor changed in its value on a specific date in time (*the effective date*) without monies invested in improvements, there are limitations to the fixed asset. However, the market can offer opportunities to generate a higher property value if the market participants accept or demand additional improvements. One of the major challenges in considering the addition of a unit is the typical practice of appraisers who have their focus on current market value with little thought of future, as real estate markets are cyclical and constantly changing.

Investors who are seeking to increase their profit face challenges when considering adding improvements to the subject.

Challenges with making improvements include the:

1. Cost
2. Depreciation schedule

At some point in time, the improvements that may generate more income can be a short-lived period of time. If the investment of additional items has a *negative* impact, then there is a decrease in return. Conversely, if the investment has a *positive* impact, then there is an increase in return.

This economic principle of increasing and decreasing returns defines the need for improvements installed to have a positive impact on the overall return of the investment. Over time, the cost of maintaining the item will ultimately create a *decrease to the return*.

Opportunity Costs

A principle closely related to the principle of substitution is the principle of opportunity costs. The principle of opportunity costs communicates the reasoning of the buyer/investor's choice to purchase that specific property. Through careful analysis, comparing all other opportunities, the decision to purchase or invest is the action of the investor's *belief that this specific investment will offer the greatest opportunity for the return on and of the monies invested.* Once the action is taken to buy the property, the buyer removes himself from the investors' market pool. The investment decision is the investor's conclusion that this one investment will return the highest yield in exchange for the monies spent to acquire the property. Their decision to buy and remove themselves from the investors' market pool eliminates the possibility of all other opportunities on that effective date.

When analyzing rates of return (a necessary requirement in order to attract capital), the comparison of prospective rates of return for alternative investment opportunities is reviewed. The conclusion of the analysis supports the appraiser's judgment of the appropriate yield rate.

Principles of Marketability

The Principles of Marketability include:

- Supply and Demand
- Change
- Externalities
- Competition
- Integration, Equilibrium, Decline, and Renewal
- Conformity
- Marginal Utility
- Progression and Regression

Principles of Marketability Highlights

The marginal utility principle listed under the Principles of Marketability is highlighted and summarized to provide a further exploration of how this principle relates to the Income Approach.

Marginal Utility

This principle is closely akin to the principle of contribution because it relates to a component's value being determined in the marketplace. The economic concept is that *value* and *utility* have a relationship. Finding marginal utility starts with a couple of steps:

1. The worth of the item begins with the market's perception of the component's utility.
2. Once the utility has been identified and defined, the second reaction to measure is the worth of that utility by measuring the demand of the utility.

When the demand for something of value exceeds the supply for the item, the value will have a higher degree of marginal utility. Conversely, when the supply of the item is greater than the demand for the item, the degree of marginal utility is lower.

Example

A two-story, four-unit property with a deck on the second floor has no stairs for outdoor access from the first level. The utility of the deck could be physically enhanced with an addition of an external staircase. However, it's not necessary, as the second level can be reached by going inside and taking the stairs up to the deck. The cost to construct an external staircase would be $2,500.

Under the principle of contribution, the worth of decks in the market on upper-level dwellings of similar size ranges from $1,500 to $2,000. Because there is no identifiable distinction between those upper decks with stairs and those without stairs, the conclusion is that stairs being added to the upper deck will have a low degree of marginal utility. The value of the property having an upper deck with stairs is *not* equal or greater than the demand.

Summary Overview of the Appraisal Process

The appraisal of real property rights is a progressive critical thinking process. As stated previously, there is a sequential, systematic, process of solving the problem for value. That process for the real property appraiser who adheres to a professional set of standards will generally by law, by choice, or by agreement follow the Uniform Standards of Professional Appraisal Practice (USPAP). Those copyrighted professional standards can be obtained by going to www.appraisalfoundation.org. These standards are published by The Appraisal Foundation (TAF) as a work of the Appraisal Standards Board (ASB). The chart, on the next page, is a summary overview of the steps in the Appraisal Process.

For income properties, there will be varied financial analyses performed in the data collection and analysis stage and the conclusions of those analyses will provide the appraiser sufficient information to develop what is known as a **Net Operating Income Statement** (NOI).

Net Operating Income

There is an order to processing income from rent to cash before debt.

Annual Market Rent + Annual Other Income = PGI – Vacancy and Credit Loss = EGI ↓

EGI – Fixed Expenses – Variable Operating Expenses – Reserves for Replacements = NOI

Potential Gross Income

This is an annualized income for a property derived from the market level gross rent plus other income, assuming no vacancy or interruption of the rent from the units or space. Other income could come from vending machines, parking space rental, etc. The use of PGI is appropriate in market value appraisals as well as with some other types of value. When the leased fee estate is being appraised, contract rent (sometimes referred to as "scheduled" income) is used. Contract rent reflects the actual amount being generated under the current lease terms.

Potential Gross Income broken down can be explained as follows:

- **Potential** is used because it assumes no interruption of monies *potentially* that can be obtain from leasing the unit or space, based upon a survey of similar rentals in the market. This is what the property could rent for if available for rental on the effective date.

- **Gross** in this context means without expense.

- **Income** in this line item refers to cash.

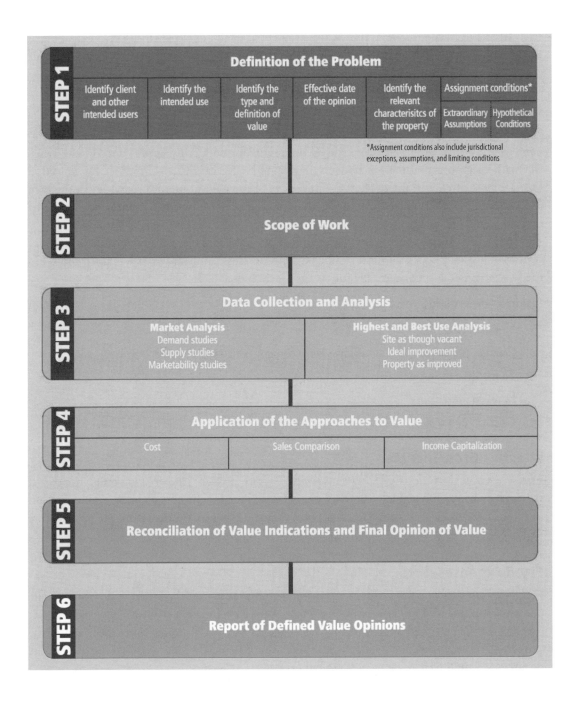

Vacancy Loss

When analyzing NOI, an estimated rate of vacancy is considered. Losses due to vacancy are usually based on a percentage (rather than a flat dollar amount) of the PGI. The percentage applied in the appraiser's analysis of the subject's PGI is derived from information obtained through the property owner, analysis of the leases or rent roll, and from market data of other similar properties.

A vacancy rate is *a percentage rate for all units comprised of the total number of unrented days divided by the total number of rentable days in a year*. A vacancy rate estimated by the appraiser for determining a dollar amount of vacancy loss should always reflect market level when using

PGI. Therefore, while the appraiser will certainly examine an actual or historic vacancy rate of the subject, that data must be tested against data obtained from the market to determine relevance.

Credit Loss

Credit loss is *an amount stated as a percent or a dollar amount reflecting the risk anticipated for nonpayment of rent by tenants.* An estimated amount for **collection loss** is appropriate when the market supports that there is evidence in the market for its use. An allowance for collection losses is most often warranted when the property is large with numerous rental units, or when it is commonplace for renters to vacate without paying the rent owed. This information can be derived from surveys similar to that which was performed to derive a market vacancy rate. In most residential assignments of smaller income properties, applying a number or percentage for collection loss may be less common. When a collection loss is warranted, it is applied to PGI in the same manner as the percentage for vacancy loss.

Examples of credit loss include:

- Unpaid rents
- Charges for collection (including labor costs for collecting the debt)
- Non-sufficient funded checks
- Bank charges
- Eviction costs, etc.

Effective Gross Income

Effective Gross Income (EGI) is what is often referred to as "the true income" because it represents what cash is actually expected under professional management prior to the payment outflow of expenses. It is from this standpoint that the expenses for operating the property are deducted.

Fixed Expenses

Fixed expenses are *expenses that are set or required to be paid yearly.* The expenses do not fluctuate and are not influenced by vacancy or credit loss. A fixed expense is a cost that is a fixed amount for the fiscal year charged to the property regardless of whether or not income is received by the property. Property taxes and property insurance would be fixed expenses that, regardless of the occupancy, would have to be paid as annual expenses.

Variable Operating Expenses

The term "**variable operating**" defines *the fluctuation of costs throughout the fiscal year in operating and maintaining the property.* A variable operating expense is reported as a sum for the fiscal year. It is here where the appraiser is most vulnerable in developing this expenditure cost. Many property owners will have used the monies from the real estate income for their personal or other business. In many cases an amount is deducted for depreciation of the asset. This type of book depreciation cannot be considered in this expenditure.

The types of variable operating expenses will vary with different property types and with lease terms of responsible parties. Regardless of the variance of expenses it is a cost charged to the income stream to ensure that the cash flow will not be interrupted.

Reserves for Replacements

This last segmented charge to the income stream is for assurance of capital in the event a short-lived component needs replacement. The judgment of whether or not the item should be included in the reserved contribution to capital (reserves for replacement) brings about the necessity of the item to maintain the occupancy and renew or continue the economic life. Criteria to establish the need to have (and use) capital replacement is based on:

- Appropriateness as a capital replacement versus an operating expense or capital improvement
- Necessity and urgency of the need

NOI – Net Operating Income

The **Net Operating Income** (NOI) is *the net income remaining before any income taxes or debt service*. It is an assumed cash profit (prior to taxes and any other indebtedness tied to the owner's asset portfolio such as a lien or mortgage) from the right of ownership exchanged for the benefit of receiving rent.

Chapter Summary

1. Income properties are investments that thread the individual investor, whether the owner or interested purchaser, the tenant, the licensed agent, and the real property appraiser together. Each has a perspective that has a focus on the income production.

2. Certain economic principles are necessary to understand regardless of the perspective. Income production and the marketability of the income property are directly connected to known economic principles.

3. Appraisal of real property rights is a sequential, logical process that begins with understanding the problem of value to be solved.

4. The Income Approach begins with developing a Net Operating Income Statement. The NOI, similar to the appraisal process, is a sequential, orderly, step-by-step process. The end result is an assumed cash remainder after the rent has been properly processed for the anticipated expenses associated with a maintained and professionally managed tenant-occupied property.

Chapter Quiz

1. *What best describes the category of expense in a developed NOI that recognizes available monies for components that have outlived their life expectancy?*

   A. Fixed
   B. Property Management
   C. Reserves for replacement
   D. Variable Operating

2. *The need to consider making an improvement to an existing property will include in the decision the cost of the improvement and the term additional monies can be received for making that improvement. The economic principle that speaks to that income decision is the principle of*

   A. the agents of production.
   B. balance.
   C. increasing and decreasing returns.
   D. substitution.

3. *In the appraisal process, the elements of problem identification lead to the next step in the process, which is*

   A. acceptance of the appraisal assignment.
   B. deciding the highest and best use.
   C. determining the scope of work.
   D. developing the applicable approaches to value

4. *A land theory that also plays a critical role as a step in the appraisal process is the principle of*

   A. anticipation.
   B. contribution.
   C. highest and best use.
   D. substitution.

5. *Adjustments made to comparable transactions are based on the perception of value to the market participants and not the cost. The economic principle representing that truth is the principle of*

   A. contribution.
   B. depreciation.
   C. highest and best use.
   D. increasing and decreasing returns.

6. *When an investor purchases a property and by that action, removes himself from the buying pool for other investment properties that may be also attractive, the investor is experiencing the principle of*

   A. anticipation.
   B. competition.
   C. increasing and decreasing returns.
   D. opportunity costs.

7. *Expenses that are annually deducted and set for the year regardless of the income received are known as*

   A. fixed expenses.
   B. reserves for replacements.
   C. scope of work.
   D. vacancy and credit loss.

8. *A property contains four units that rent monthly for $800 each. Vacancy and credit loss is 4% of the Potential Gross Income. Other income is not available on this property type. What is the Potential Gross Income?*

   A. $3,200
   B. $18,432
   C. $36,864
   D. $38,400

9. *What is the Effective Gross Income of a property that generates $40,000 annual rent, with other income reported annually at $2,000, and has a vacancy and credit loss of 5%?*

   A. $38,000
   B. $39,900
   C. $40,000
   D. $42,000

10. *An investor seeks to yield 10% on his investment. He believes if he can purchase a property for $150,000, at the end of five years, he can sell the property for $241,600. What economic principle best describes his offer of $150,000?*

    A. anticipation
    B. contribution
    C. opportunity costs
    D. substitution

Chapter 2:
Analysis of Gross Income

Chapter Objectives

After completing this chapter, you will be able to:

- Contrast the difference between contract rent and market rent.
- Define how to analyze market rent.
- Identify how to make adjustments for a market rent analysis.
- Describe how to properly compose a market rent schedule.
- Define the roles of vacancy and credit loss and other income in the development of Effective Gross Income.
- Identify how to process Gross Market Rent, Potential Gross Income, and Effective Gross Income.

Contract Rent The agreed amount that has enforceable terms between the tenant (lessee) and the owner (lessor).

Effective Rent The residual of rent after any rental concessions.

Market Rent The amount documented to represent the central tendency of behavior between knowledgeable lessors and lessees.

Key Terms

Chapter Introduction

Processing gross income for residential income-producing properties isn't simply a quick review of the houses that have tenant occupancy. Gross rent impacts the gross income that can only be credibly developed once carefully analyzed as of an effective date and correlated to a specific property type. Adjustments for amenities and concessions must be considered. The ability to process gross income from a gross monthly rent to an effective gross income is vital when the Income Approach is being developed. This chapter focuses on understanding the various types of gross income and how they may be influenced.

The reliability of the Income Approach is rooted in the credibility of the indications revealed in the development of the Income Approach. There are two (2) main components to this process:

1. The income, whether gross or net

2. The **divisor** (known as *a capitalization rate*) or a **multiplier** (*an alternative method to valuing income based on the gross income*).

This chapter will place its focus on identifying in the market a rent that meets the needs of the problem to be solved, when market value is the solution required by the client. It is important to keep in mind that market value is the type of value most often sought by the lender (known as the mortgagee), but any encumbrance (impediment to the value being sought) must also be identified. When a property has a long-term lease (generally considered 20+ years), there is an encumbrance to the market value and the **leased-fee interest** (*the value based on the contract rent*) will be necessary to process and consider as an impact to the **market value** (*a value based in part on the market rent and not contract rent*).

Most residential income-producing properties are leased for six (6), nine (9), or twelve (12) months. Although technically the leases may be an encumbrance to the market value, their leased-fee interest is short-term. In many cases when the demand for the property is high, the investor will treat that short-term period as a *transition to the goal of maximizing the income* and purchase the property in spite of any contract rent being lower than current market rent. In some instances, if there is a default clause in the contract, the penalty for the default will be paid by the investor in order to expedite a market rent to be paid by the tenant in place or to have the tenant released by the contract obligations and relocate if she is not willing to pay the rent increase.

To form a conclusion of the market rent, the investor should seek assistance from either a licensed property manager or licensed real estate agent, and have that confirmed by a market rent survey by the appraiser. Very often the appraiser and licensed agent work together so that any analysis required by the investor, performed by the appraiser, can be assisted with information gathered in part by the property manager(s) in the market area. It will sometimes occur that *both* the property manager and the appraiser will conduct separate analyses. The key to the reliability is in the strength of the credibility of rent analysis conducted by the professionals involved.

Gross Rent: A Varied Perspective

Measuring gross rent may be viewed differently depending on the *individual* seeking the gross rent. Some examples reveal the differences:

- The **investor** will push toward seeking the *highest rent* they can command. Remember the investor has a desired yield: *The greater the amount of the rent charged brings that yield into closer reach.*

- The **leasing agent** will work towards filling the available space, because his commission is most often paid on leased space, not the space to be leased.

- The **tenant** will obviously consider the location, what the space can provide, and the amenities connected to the rent.

- The **appraiser** may be required to consider the contract rent and value the property from a "leased fee" perspective and the conclusion of rent from the negotiated rent between and the offeror/lessor (whether direct or the result of a leasing agent).

Contract rent is *the agreed amount that has enforceable terms between the tenant (lessee) and the owner (lessor).* The strength of any contract is in direct proportion to its **enforceability**. **Market rent** is *that amount documented to represent the central tendency of behavior between knowledgeable lessors and lessees.* **Effective rent** is *the residual of rent after any rental concessions. It can be more or less than the actual rent stated.*

Example:

- If a pet fee was added to the rent in the amount of $50 per month, the contract would cite the rental rate for the space at $800 per month, but the effective rent would be $850.

- In some cases, the need to improve occupancy creates a rental concession that may involve, for example, $100 off the rent with a lease scheduled for one (1) year. The contract rent will show $800 per month, but the concession clause will reduce the rent to an effective rent of $791.67 ($9,600 - $100 concession ÷ 12 months = $791.67).

√ **Note:** An important factor that must be at the forefront is the gross rent must be linked to the property type and the security of the continuity of that income must also be tendered with the **quantity**, **quality,** and **durability** of the income.

Measuring Gross Rent

Most tenants, known as lessees, will report their rent in terms of space. Consider the example below from a residential income property tenant perspective. Design, style, and lifestyle factors may play a role in the demand.

Scenario: The appraiser interviewed the tenant to identify demand and the role it plays with the tenant. The tenant responded *"There are two-bedroom units available in a townhouse design, which includes a small seating area and a postage-stamp yard in the rear. Other two-bedroom options are available in a flat design on either a lower level or on an upper level. I considered the advantages of each one.*

Townhouse Design

In the townhouse, I would need to climb stairs every time I went to the bedroom, but the stairs would increase my feelings of security. In the event the unit was broken into, it would be easy to hear someone using the staircase. The downside is a potential lack of privacy, because bi-weekly, the groundskeeper will be back and forth in my yard. I love the fireplace though, as it is located next to French doors looking out to the small yard.

Flat Design

The flat design has an upper-level that would increase my feelings of security, but carrying groceries and bags up and down stairs would be a hassle. In addition, on the upper level, the outside is limited to a small balcony that could hold two chairs and a few potted plants. There's also a restriction on outdoor cooking.

Rent Comparisons

*The rent for the townhouse is $125 **more** per month than the flat design. The flat design on the upper level can be rented for $25 a month less than the lower level. If I rent a house in the same area, yard care would be my responsibility, the security would be more vulnerable, and the rent would be about $200 **more** a month. I also would not have the fireplace or upgraded kitchen furnished with all of the appliances."*

At that point, the tenant has chosen a location and is now wrestling with the added amenity of the *floorplan*. The struggle of the decision weighs the perceived outdoor access and the security of living upstairs with a lower rent, against the lower level and the difference in lifestyle.

There is also a consideration of the difference between the single-family property management vs. onsite management of the apartment and townhome. When vacancy is stable and tenants can consider the design of a property, the leasing agent, the investor, and the tenant have formed a market opinion about the rental unit.

This illustration gives evidence that for each property, whether residential or non-residential, prospective tenants (lessees) make decisions through comparisons that could impact a property's potential to generate income. Even within the residential income property type, impact can be identified from the comparisons made within the various residential property types. In community rentals (apartments, townhomes, etc.), some privacy is sacrificed for the advantages of onsite management.

Case Study: Conducting a Survey of Market Rent of the Single-Family Dwelling

The investor of a newly renovated single-family property has hired a licensed real estate agent to lease the dwelling. The investor wants to ask for a monthly gross rent of $900 and a one-year lease. The subject is a 20-year detached single-family dwelling that includes:

- Two (2) Bedrooms
- Two (2) baths
- Central air conditioning
- 1,150 sq. ft. of gross leasable area (GLA)
- Single car garage
- Kitchen (including range, fan/hood, dishwasher, and refrigerator)
- No pets permitted
- Unfenced yard

The agent set forth to perform a rental analysis of the market.

Item	Rental #1	Rental #2	Rental #3	Rental #4
Gross Monthly Rent	$825	$1,000	$875	$1,100
Bedrooms/Baths	2 Bed, 1.1 Bath	3 Bed, 2.1 Bath	2 Bed, 2 Bath	3 Bed, 2 Bath
Kitchen Appliance	Range, Fan/Hood, Ref	Range, Fan/Hood, DW, Ref	Range, Fan/Hood, DW, Ref	Range, Fan/Hood, DW, Ref
Heat & Air	Wall Unit Air	Central Air	Central Air	Central Air
Car Storage	Sngl Carport	Sngl Garage	Sngl Carport	Dbl Garage
Pets Allowed	Yes; addt'l $200 deposit, limit 2 pets, non-refund	Yes, addt'l $200 deposit, limit 2 pets, non-refund	No pets allowed.	Yes, addt'l $200 deposit, limit 2 pets, non-refund
GLA	1,100	1,150	1,200	1,400
Fence	No	Yes	No	Yes
Terms	9 months $400 deposit	12 months $500 deposit	9 months $450 deposit	12 months $500 deposit

Apply Your Knowledge 2.1

1. **What is the central tendency about the allowance of pets?**

   _____

   _____

   a) **Is there a rental difference per unit or a deposit difference?**

   _____

2. **Based upon the data analyzed, what is the rent per :**

Sq. Ft. Gross Living Area	#1 _____	#2 _____	#3 _____	#4 _____
Each Bedroom	#1 _____	#2 _____	#3 _____	#4 _____

3. **Is there a central tendency of air conditioning?**

   _____

4. **Are the investor's desires for rent and terms of rental supported in the market?**

   _____

   _____

5. **What is a reasonable monthly market rent that would secure a qualified tenant?**

   _____

   _____

Adjusting for Amenities

Conducting a rent survey also requires separating additional services or amenities in order to identify the *actual gross income* from the *gross leasable area*. For example, one way a property owner may enjoy additional income is to pay a lower per-unit rate for the utilities and then charge them back into the rent to the tenant. The tenant will actually be paying a higher rate than the property owner, but may prefer not having to come up with the deposit and monthly bill obligation. If the normal utility monthly bill is $100, but the tenant can pay an additional $75 a month for rent, then the outflow and convenience to the tenant for the amenity is a *benefit* to the tenant. The owner of the property may be able to purchase the units for a cost of $60 a month.

Although $15 a month may not seem worth the paperwork, if the apartment complex has 200 units even with a vacancy of 5% the owner is earning an additional $2,850 per month or **$34,200** per year.

Case Study: Recognizing the Impact of Concessions on Gross Income

Gross rent may be quoted at one stated, fixed amount, but under the principle of competition, there may be a need to offer a concession to "seal the deal." For example, an owner of a 400-unit complex may be competing with a newly constructed complex in the same neighborhood. Let's say a newer competing complex is offering a unit of the same size and number of bedrooms/baths for $650 monthly rent with a nine-month lease. The owner of the older complex would most likely want to charge the same monthly rent, but may offer another incentive to absorb any vacant spaces.

To understand the feasibility of this plan, let's deconstruct the reasoning of the older complex owner.

If the older complex offers for a 12-month lease monthly rent at $650 and a 90-day discount:

- For the first month: Discount of **$100** (or a 1st month rent payment of **$550**)
- For the second month: Discount of **$75** (or a 2nd month rent payment of **$575**)
- For the third month: Discount of **$50** (or a 3rd month rent payment of **$600**)
- For the remaining nine months: Rent of **$650**

This incentive may be the concession to get the tenant to sign the lease.

So, what is the true rental income of the older complex if the discounts are factored in?

Annual Rent of Unit with No Discounts

	$ 650	(Rent Schedule)
x	12	(Amount of Months of Rent)
=	**$7,800**	**(Annual Rent)**

Annual Adjusted Rent of Unit with Discounts

	$7,800	(Annual Rent)
-	$225	(Monthly Rent Discounts: $100 + $75 + $50)*
=	**$7,575**	**(Annual Income Adjusted)**

Adjusted Monthly Rent after Discounts

	$7,575	(Annual Adjusted Rent)
÷	12	(Number of Months in Annual Rental Period)
=	**$631.25**	**(Adjusted Monthly Rent)**

* **Annual rent discounts** are calculated using a straight-line method. Straight-line, in this instance, occurs when the amount of discount is a fixed amount per period, over time.

Taking on a Higher Vacancy vs. Discounting Annual Rent

If the current market rate of vacancy and credit loss is 5%, but the competition of the new complex is believed to be the reason for the subject's vacancy of **8%**, then the concession is a matter of money. At an increase of 3% of vacancy, the owner of the older complex must consider the loss:

- **Vacancy of 5% Loss**

  $650 x 12 Months x 400 Units = $3,120,000 - $156,000 (Market Rate of Vacancy @ 5%)
   = $2,964,000

- **Vacancy of 8% Loss**

  $650 x 12 Months x 400 Units = $3,120,000 - $249,600 (Market Rate of Vacancy @ 8%)
   = $2,870,400

- **Discounted Annual Rent with a Vacancy of 5% Loss**

  $631.25 x 12 Months x 400 Units = $3,030,000 – $151,500 (Market Rate of Vacancy @ 5%)
   = $2,878,500

So, without the incentive, the loss due to vacancy is estimated at **$249,600** (8% x $3,120,000).

With the incentive the loss of income at a market rate of 5% is estimated at **$151,500**. This rate can be found by performing the following calculation:

	$3,030,000	($631.25 monthly discounted rent x 400 units x 12 months)
x	5%	(market rate of vacancy)
=	**$151,500**	(loss of income due to vacancy)

Higher Vacancy vs. Discounting Annual Rent

The cost of the discounting is already in the adjusted discounted monthly rent. The total loss is the difference between the income prior to newer building and the adjusted annual gross income less vacancy. It can be calculated as follows:

- $650 x 12 Months x 400 Units = $3,120,000 - $156,000 (Market Rate of Vacancy @ 5%)
  = **$2,964,000**

- $631.25 x 12 Months x 400 Units = $3,030,000 - $151,500 (Market Rate of Vacancy @ 5%)
  = **$2,878,500**

	$2,964,000.00	(Non-Discounted Annual Rent 5% Vacancy Loss)
-	$2,878,500.00	(Discounted Annual Rent 5% Vacancy Loss)
=	**$ 85,500.00**	(Loss due to External Forces of Increased Supply)

Without the concession that loss would have been:

	$2,964,000	(Gross Income after Vacancy of 5%)
-	$2,870,400	(Gross Income Unadjusted with Vacancy of 8%)
=	**$93,600**	(Loss if the rent is not adjusted)

Either way you look at it, the newer complex now poses an external impact on the cash flow. However, by adjusting the rent with an incentive, the tenancy is committed to a longer term and, therefore, the loss is not as difficult to absorb ($93,600 - $85,500 = **$8,100**). The next topic in this chapter will explore how a property owner can also consider supporting the income cash flow with an investment in renovations to possibly add to the cash flow without increasing the rent.

Vacancy and Credit Loss

Vacancy Factor, Rate, and Space

Remember, vacancy means *not utilized*. A **vacancy factor** is *the amount of gross revenue that pro forma income statements anticipate will be lost due to unleased space*. Most vacancy factors are expressed as percentages of the total rentable square footage that is available for rent. The vacancy rate is a calculation that is used to show the relationship of total available space when compared to total inventory of space. Vacant space relates to the existing tenant space that is currently being marketed for lease. It excludes available space for any subletting that's allowed and common area.

Formula: Vacant Gross Leasable Space ÷ Total Inventory = **Vacancy Rate**

Vacancy can be either:

1. Physical
2. Financial

Physical vacancy is *the number of units unoccupied divided by the total number of units available*. **Financial vacancy** *reports the income impact of the property being valued*.

Table A

Physical Vacancy			Economic/Financial Vacancy	Calculations
Total Possible Units Available	150		Total Possible Units	150
Total PGI $1,119,000			20 (3) Bedroom GMR	$ 180,000 PGI
Or $7,460 per Unit			$750 pUnit pMonth x 12	+
			80 (2) Bedroom GMR	$ 624,000 PGI
			$650 pUnit pMonth x 12	+
			50 (1) Bedroom GMR	$ 315,000 PGI
			$525 pUnit pMonth x 12	**$1,119,000 PGI**
Number of Units Vacant over the Year	5		Vacant Units	
			4 (3) Bedroom for 3 months	$ 9,000
			4 x $750 x 3	+
			7 (2) Bedroom for 2 months	$ 9,100
			7 x $650 x 2	+
			2 (1) Bedroom for 4 months	$ 4,200
			2 x $525 x 4	**$ 22,300 Vacancy**
Physical Vacancy Factor	*3.3%*		*Economic Vacancy*	*2%*

Credit Loss

Credit loss is not tied to the physical vacancy factor. This type of loss is part of the economic vacancy which is over and above those units unoccupied. Examples of credit loss include:

- Unpaid rents
- Charges for collection including labor costs for collecting the debt
- Non-sufficient funded checks
- Bank charges
- Eviction costs, etc.

Few appraisers actually gather this information, which can, in many cases, add significant amounts of loss. For example, if the credit loss was 1% of the occupied income on Table A, the cost would be as follows:

	$1,119,000	(Potential Gross Income)
-	22,300	(Actual Economic Impact of Physical Vacancy)
=	**$1,096,700**	(Income Prior to Expenses and Credit Loss)
x	.01	(Credit Loss)
=	**$ 10,967**	(Loss of Rental Income Due to Credit Loss)

Vacancy and credit loss in this scenario present a calculation as follows:

	$22,300	(Vacancy loss of income due to unoccupied units)
+	10,967	(Credit loss 1% of occupied units)
=	$33,267	(Total income lost to vacancy and credit)
÷	$1,119,000	(PGI)
=	**0.0297**	**or 2.97% (Total Economic Vacancy and Credit Loss)**

Other Income

As stated previously, of the four (4) basic types of gross income, the gross monthly rent begins the process of developing the income from a gross to a net operating income.

Four Types of Gross Income

There are four (4) types of gross income, listed as follows:

1. **Gross Monthly Rent**
2. **Gross Annual Rent**
3. **Potential Gross Income** (annualized rent + addition of other income)
4. **Effective Gross Income** (the true income prior to expenses)

To develop the gross monthly rent into an annual rent, the gross monthly rent amount must be multiplied by twelve (12) months. It's very important for appraisers to analyze market rent with *a market value standard of measure*.

- When the type of value being analyzed is market value, the income must be based on the market or economic rent.

- If the property is being valued subject to a lease, the actual contract (scheduled) rent is used.

Other income is income that is derived from "non-realty" venues. There are categories of other income that enable the user of the appraisal report the necessary understanding of why that income had to be considered in the appraisal. Other income is necessary to consider when *the voidance of that income will injure the occupancy of the building.*

Categories of Other Income

There are several categories of other income. These categories will be explored and discussed in this section.

Contractual Income

This type of other income is generated from coin-operated equipment. The general method of how this additional income is contracted is an agreement between the coin-operated equipment vendor, who supplies and services the machines, and the property owner. The contract typically calls for a splitting of the profits with the owner.

Example

Cost of machine:	$1,500	
Life expectancy of the machine:	5	years
Supplies for the machine:	$54	per week
Maintenance costs:	$25	twice monthly
Projected weekly income from the machine	$100	
	x 4.3	weeks per month
	$430	per month
Less monthly supplies of machine:	- 232.20	($54.00 x 4.3)
Less monthly maintenance:	- 50.00	($25.00 x 2)
Less straight line depreciation of the machine:	- 25.00	per month ($1,500 cost/60 month life expectancy)
Net Profit before Taxes:	$122.80	
Percentage Split	x 30%	
	= $ 36.84	projected gross per month
Projected Gross to Property Owner	$36.84	projected per month
Divided by projected monthly Gross Income	÷ $430.00	
Percentage split of gross income stated in contract	8.57%	

Optional Income

Another way a property can generate optional income is by making personal property, such as equipment and furniture, available for tenants to rent.

Example

The gross monthly rent for each unit of a 100-unit apartment complex is $650 without a refrigerator. With a refrigerator, the gross monthly rent is $660. The vacancy rate overall last year was 4%. The percentage of tenants who chose to rent with a refrigerator was 70%. With such a high tenant demand, it's reasonable to conclude this other income is necessary to maintain a stabilized occupancy.

What is the other income associated with this option?"

The following calculation reveals the solution to this problem.

Step 1: Find the demand for units with refrigerators

	100	(units)
x	96%	(occupancy)
=	96%	(occupancy) (100% occupancy – 4% vacancy)
x	70%	(of occupants take this option)
=	**67.2**	(round to 67 units)

Step 2: Calculate the optional income from this demand

	67	(units)
x	$10.00	(per month)
=	$670.00	
x	12	(months)
=	**$8,040.00**	

√ **Note:** This income is valued prior to the costs of the appliances, maintenance, and depreciation.

Parking Income

Where land is scarce, densely developed, and heavily trafficked, there will often be an additional charge for parking on site. Parking income can come from the tenants in a commercial or residential building or from others. When this income is generated from sources other than the tenants, the appraiser will have to ensure sufficient analyses and review of the income statements are made to accurately calculate the income necessary to maintain the occupancy.

Most often, the tenants' needs are identified to ensure the lease and parking meet their demand. For example, businesses that rely heavily on retail trade will need more space than professional offices.

Resale of Utilities Income

Building owners may generate additional income by reselling utilities, such as water, cable television, or electricity. They will use one meter for the entire complex. The amount that is charged to the tenants is not broken out separately for the tenant—it's made part of the tenant's *gross rent*. The owner will purchase the utility service at a wholesale price and then resell the utility to the tenants. They can charge either a *flat fee* or a *proportionate fee* according to the size of the leasable unit.

√ **Note:** This type of other income is typically seen in property types such as office buildings, mobile home parks, and shopping centers.

Service Income

Certain services, such as janitorial, personal shopping, or childcare are often demanded in densely developed areas where the pace of life is fast and time has a significant value to the tenants. The property owner engages in a contract with a company to provide these services, receiving a portion of the fee charged in the form of a commission. Scrutiny of the tenant's lifestyle to identify the demand for those services would be necessary to support the need for this type of other income.

Investors with minimal land seeking a manner to maximize their value will often turn to the possibility of converting part of their common area or leasable space into generating other income. The principle of increasing and decreasing returns and the principle of contribution play important roles in determining other income. An investor must consider the current use of a space and the income it produces as Gross Leasable Area (GLA) or Gross Building Area (GBA) before adding a service for his tenants. This will require close scrutiny to determine if the renovation would be economically viable.

Other Income and Residential Income Property Types

Residential income property types can be the detached single-family home, the duplex (two units), four-plex (four units), or other small-unit property types. It can also be the 500-unit apartment complex. The ability of the property to earn other income, as stated previously, is tied to the need to maintain the occupancy. In smaller one-to-four-unit property types, there is generally not an opportunity to earn any real additional income, except through utilities, and then it may not be worth the time and effort. Generally speaking, other income is reserved for the larger unit property types.

Earlier, the topic of the external influence of a newer complex required maneuvering to capture the tenants who may choose the newer development over the older one. For a property with 400 units, one way to consider generating other income without too much cost is by offering covered parking or janitorial care service. Depending on the tenant demographic and the location, that opportunity may afford the owner to pick up additional income, further compensating for the external impact of the newer unit.

Developing Potential Gross Income and Effective Gross Income

Licensees must understand that income doesn't have to come solely from the gross leasable area or unit. Licensees must also understand the role of vacancy and credit loss, and the two types of gross annual income that can be developed to develop a reasonable income analysis.

Two Types of Annual Gross Income

1. **Potential Gross Income**: Potential Scheduled Gross Income is the annual rent without consideration for vacancy and credit loss and without consideration of the other potential scheduled gross income.

2. **Potential Gross Income**: Potential Gross Income is the annualized rent and income from other sources without consideration for vacancy and credit loss.

√ **Caution!** It's critical that these income streams are processed in the proper order as their relationship to their value can be identified through multipliers, a subject to be discussed in the next chapter.

Apply Your Knowledge: Discussion Practice

Based on the following scenario develop the gross income.

The subject is a twenty (20)-unit small apartment complex. Each two (2)-bedroom, two (2)-bath unit rents for $750 per month. There is a laundry hook-up in each unit. For an additional $40 per month, the tenants can use the workout room, which has exercise equipment. The annual income received for those additional services available was $3,360. The vacancy and credit loss was equal to 4% of the annualized rent.

1. What is the Gross Monthly Rent? _____

2. What is the Gross Annual Rent? _____

3. What is the Potential Gross Income? _____

4. What is the Effective Gross Income? _____

√ **Note:** Order of processing the gross income is critical. Other income represents occupied income. Had the vacancy been applied after other income, then the other income would have suffered vacancy twice.

Chapter Summary

1. Gross income can be reported monthly or annually.

2. The only gross income that is affected by vacancy and credit loss is Effective Gross Income.

3. Potential Gross Income is the sum of the annual rents and reported other income generated from "non-realty" venues.

4. The sequencing and order of processing gross income is critical when developing a net operating income statement.

Chapter Quiz

1. **What is the potential gross income of a four-unit residential property that rents for $675 per month and has a 5% vacancy?**

   A. $2,592
   B. $2,700
   C. $31,104
   D. $32,400

2. **Other income is**

   A. automatically deducted from the expense analysis.
   B. expected on all income properties.
   C. most often seen in multiple residential units such as larger unit property types.
   D. not considered part of the NOI.

3. **What is the Effective Gross Income of a duplex that rents for $800 per unit per month and has an annualized vacancy and credit loss of 4%?**

   A. $1,536
   B. $1,600
   C. $18,432
   D. $19,170

4. **Vacancy is a(n) _____ loss of income, whereas credit loss is a(n) _____ loss.**

   A. external, internal
   B. financial, physical
   C. internal, external
   D. physical, financial

5. **If a forty-unit complex derived part of its income from the $500 per unit per month rent and $2,900 per year from housecleaning services, what is the Effective Gross Income if vacancy and credit loss are 5% of the annualized rent?**

   A. $230,900
   B. $242,900
   C. $359,200
   D. $400,356

6. **The residual rent after considering any rental concessions is known as**

   A. effective rent.
   B. eventual rent.
   C. financial rent.
   D. structural rent.

7. **Leasing agents are most often paid a commission based on the**

   A. flat fee per month until the units reach a market rate of occupancy.
   B. half of the first month's rent and half of the deposit.
   C. leased space for which they were responsible in securing a lease.
   D. terms set by their local Boards of Realtors.

8. **Investors with minimal land seeking a manner to maximize their value will often turn to the possibility of converting part of their common area or leasable space into generating other income. Which principle plays a role in the consideration of other income?**

   A. agents of production and highest and best use
   B. highest and best use and change
   C. increasing and decreasing returns and contribution
   D. substitution and anticipation

9. **All gross income processed into an NOI must begin with**

   A. an analysis of the vacancy and credit loss due to poor management.
   B. a lease analysis in a market value.
   C. the market rent survey for market rent to reconcile gross monthly rent.
   D. the target contract rent from the lessor.

10. **The credit loss is $700 for the year in an eight-unit building that rents for $900 per unit. What is the percent of vacancy and credit loss for this income property if one unit remains vacant for six months and another unit remains vacant for three months?**

    A. 4%
    B. 6%
    C. 8%
    D. 10%

Chapter 3

Multipliers: Converting Gross Income into Value

Chapter Objectives

After completing this chapter, you will be able to:

- Identify how to perform multiplier capitalization.
- Describe the process of extracting and concluding market rent.
- Define risk evaluation components.
- Identify how to develop four types of multipliers.

Multiplier Capitalization A method of converting gross income into value.

Chapter Introduction

The conversion of gross income into value is a common and necessary practice in the valuation of all income properties. In residential valuation, the use of a gross rent multiplier (GRM) is a common and customary unit measure of the relationship between the gross monthly rent and the sale price. There are other gross incomes that are developed as discussed in the previous chapter. This chapter will utilize the various types of gross income streams and, through multiplier capitalization, convert the income into a value indicator.

Gross income provides the initial component of the Net Operating Income (NOI), and it can also be converted into value through multiplier capitalization. Multiplier capitalization has a broad appeal because of its simple formula:

Gross Income X Multiplier = Value

A commonly used acronym is "VIF" (Value, Income, Factor) or "VIM" (Value, Income, Multiplier). The acronym presents the formula in a T formation for visual ease in understanding whether to divide or to multiply. You must know two of the components to get the third. For example, if you know the V, you will need to divide it by the I or M, whichever one you know.

In this example, the value and income are known amounts, so the value can be divided by the income ($560,000 ÷ $5,000) to find the gross rent multiplier. In this case, the gross rent multiplier would be 112.

Remember these sentences, and the formula works every time:

I only need to multiply the "I" and "M" to find the "V:" I X M =V.

When either the "I" or M" is missing, then I divide the "V" by either the "I" or the "M" (whichever component is present): V ÷ M = I or V ÷ I = M.

If the known is the Sale Price: $560,000 and the Income: $5,000, then the Multiplier can be found by the following equation:

(Sale Price) $560,000 ÷ $5,000 (Income) = 112 (Multiplier)

If the known is the Sale Price $560,000 and the Multiplier: 112, then the Income can be found by the following equation:

(Sale Price) $560,000 ÷ 112 (Multiplier) = $5,000 (Income)

If the known is the Income: $5,000 and the Multiplier: 112, then the Sale Price can be found by the following equation:

(Income) $5,000 X 112 (Multiplier) = $560,000 (Sale Price)

This chapter will focus on how to obtain and how to use multiplier capitalization for a simple conversion into value.

Multiplier Capitalization

Multiplier capitalization is a form of direct capitalization methodology because it assumes a long-term, unchanged future. It is preferred by many real estate professionals, as well as investors, because it is easy to understand and quick in its measure of indicated value. To ensure due diligence is being followed while performing this methodology, the real estate professional must extract the multipliers from properties with similar characteristics. Generally, this is a task done by the appraiser.

In order for the multipliers to be extracted from properties with similar characteristics, there must be **three (3) areas of comparison** made:

1. There must be similar income-to-expense ratios.
2. There must be similar land-to-building ratios.
3. The risk of the investments viewed must also be similar.

Risk Evaluation

To consider the comparative risks of other investments for multiplier extraction and application, the analyst will need to discern, and appraisers will need to communicate, the difference between the perceived risk and the actual risk of the investment.

"Risk is inherent in all business and financial activity. The evaluation of the investment risk is a key element in all estimates of wealth," Alan Greenspan, former chairman of the Federal Reserve Board, stated in a speech given in 1999, "Measuring Financial Risk in the Twenty-first Century." Mr. Greenspan said, "Any means that shifts risk from those who choose to withdraw from it to those more willing to take it on permits increased investment without significantly raising the perceived degree of discomfort from risk that the population overall experiences….The uncertainties inherent in valuations of assets and the potential for abrupt changes in perceptions of those uncertainties clearly must be adjusted by risk managers at banks and other financial intermediaries."

The determination of how much risk is reasonable depends on **two (2)** very broad factors:

1. Identifying the inherent risks of the investment
2. How willing and able the investors are to deal with the risks

There are primarily **ten (10)** characteristics of risks that impact real estate investments.

[*See October 14, 1999 Quote from Alan Greenspan, Chairman of the FRB on Measuring Financial Risk in the 21st Century.*]

Ten Characteristics of Risks that Impact Real Estate

1. **Tenant Risk:** Income properties that are multi-tenanted are less risky.
2. **Physical Obsolescence and Depreciation Risk:** Out-of-pocket capital expenditures will impact the rental income.
3. **Demand and Supply of the Specific Property Type.**
4. **Demand and Supply for Properties in Different Locations:** Identifying market conditions is critical in determining the durability of the income.

5. **Economic and Property Market Environment**: A void or stagnant economy, rental growth, debt leveraging, and pricing of surrounding similar properties listed for sale influence the quality and quantity of the income.

6. **Taxes:** Business rates and any stamp duty that may be applicable in that tax district. The higher the rates, the greater the risk to the investment.

7. **Legal and Regulatory Effects:** The constraints of planning and zoning approval as well as the impact of building codes and legal rulings such as the Landlord Tenant Act will play a role in the risk of the investment.

8. **Uncertainty of the Asset:** Value of real estate has certain risks due to the non-liquidity characteristic of real estate and market conditions that are subject to change.

9. **Yield Impacts the Risks:** Typically when the yield measures are high, there is a higher risk to the investment. The risk can be market driven as a reaction to the condition of the property or a reaction to trend changes and functional utility diminished characteristic of the property improvement. When the venture is new, the yield will be high due to the uncertainty of market acceptance.

10. **Uniqueness of Property Type:** A risk associated with certain property types requiring a below-market valuation price for quick turn-over. An example would be a recreational water park. The attractiveness of marketing this type of property will be limited to a select group of investors.

Although the majority of these risk categories can be identified by viewing the details of tenant contracts, there should be a process of reasoning that analyzes how those risks may impact the income stream and ultimately the value of the property. The analysis doesn't necessarily have to be quantitative, but it needs to be sufficiently rigorous to properly assess the risk. The ability to identify multipliers in the market will afford a measure of risk in the investment as it correlates value to a gross income.

Types of Multipliers

There are two types of multipliers that convert gross rent/income into a value:

1. Gross Rent Multiplier (GRM)

2. Gross Income Multiplier (GIM)

While the use of these multipliers is fairly simple, the derivation and application of a multiplier must be carefully performed. Therefore, there are some very important things to keep in mind when using this technique:

- The GRM and the GIM consider only the gross rent or income of the property, and, therefore, do not consider expense items.

- The GRM, and the most common form of the GIM, do not consider any losses attributable to vacancy of the living unit(s) and/or inability to collect rent.

- The market rent used in the application of a GRM to the subject property (or in the case of a GIM, total income) must reflect market level.

- The comparable properties must be very similar physically, and in lease terms and conditions.

Gross Rent Multiplier (GRM)

GRM is *a factor derived from comparable rental data, which is then used to develop an opinion of value of the subject property.* A GRM is used when the property has income that is derived only from actual rent of the living units. Although the multiplier could be expressed as either a monthly or annual factor, it is most commonly derived on a *monthly* basis for residential properties.

Developing a value opinion using the **GRM** technique of income capitalization consists of just two primary steps:

1. Determine the appropriate GRM from market data.
2. Apply the GRM to the subject's market rent to indicate a value conclusion.

While the actual steps in using a multiplier are relatively simple in application, the technique can yield misleading or false results if the data being used for the analysis is inconsistent, irrelevant, or not well analyzed.

Deriving a GRM from Market Data

Data derived from transactions of properties that were rented at the time of the sale, or shortly thereafter, reflect the expectation of the investor for the rent that is or could be collected. This is one of the more common expectations related to the principle of anticipation.

Once there is verification that the transaction is arm's-length and that the rent produced reasonably represents market level, the process of identifying a GRM from the transaction is fairly simple.

The appraiser begins the analysis by collecting information from arm's-length transactions of rental properties that are as similar to the subject as possible. Again, as mentioned earlier, a GRM can be derived and applied as either a monthly or an annual factor, using either monthly or annual rent.

√ **Note:** The monthly method will be illustrated here as it most commonly reflects the application on most residential appraisal reporting forms.

The next step is to derive the appropriate multiplier from the transaction data by using a formula known as **VIM**; *Value divided by Income equals Multiplier.*

V (sale price) ÷ I (gross monthly rent) = M (multiplier)

Let's continue on, making the assumption that the reasonable monthly market rent for the subject is $550.

For Example

Once the appraiser determines a reasonable market rent for the subject property, he researches and analyzes transaction data from the market and identifies an indicated GRM by using VIM. The following is revealed:

	Sale Price	Monthly Rent	(Formula)	GRM
1	$66,200	$530	(66,200 ÷ 530)	124.91
2	$73,000	$590	(73,000 ÷ 590)	123.73
3	$75,000	$610	(75,000 ÷ 610)	122.95
4	$65,000	$525	(65,000 ÷ 525)	123.81
5	$65,500	$500	(65,500 ÷ 500)	131.00
6	$70,000	$575	(70,000 ÷ 575)	121.74
7	$72,800	$650	(72,800 ÷ 650)	112.00
8	$68,000	$520	(68,000 ÷ 520)	130.77

In the appraiser's final analysis of the developed range of GRMs, he notes that the most common result is around 123.00, with those results ranging from just slightly less than 123.00 to the upper 123.00 range.

	Sale Price	Monthly Rent	GRM
1	$66,200	$530	124.91
2	$73,000	$590	**123.73**
3	$75,000	$610	**122.95**
4	$65,000	$525	**123.81**
5	$65,500	$500	131.00
6	$70,000	$575	121.74
7	$72,800	$650	112.00
8	$68,000	$520	130.77

In reconciling a GRM conclusion, the appraiser could choose to use 123.00 as a GRM, or probably better, place most weight on #2 (123.73) and #4 (123.81), since the GRM from those transactions most closely brackets the subject's estimated market rent of $550. For this reason, the appraiser chooses a GRM of 123.75 to apply to the subject.

Applying the GRM to the Subject

Developing a value indication for a subject property using a GRM is considered in the industry to be the simplest, if not one of the most time efficient, of the income capitalization techniques. However, as just illustrated, the simplicity and ease in this final step of the technique comes only after a very thorough analysis in determining an appropriate and relevant multiplier to apply, and a reasonable opinion of market rent to which the multiplier is applied.

To develop a value opinion using the GRM technique, the appraiser multiplies the monthly market rent of the subject by the selected multiplier.

M (multiplier) x I (monthly market rent) = V (value)

Let's illustrate this application by continuing with our previous example.

The appraiser has chosen $550 per month as a reasonable opinion of market rent for the subject property and a GRM of 123.75 to apply to the rent. Thus, the results of the appraiser's conclusions are as follows:

123.75 x $550 = $68,062.50, or rounded, $68,000

In summary, the GRM technique for use in the development of an indication of value by the income approach is the most common and frequently employed method in assignments of single-family and small residential income properties of 2-4 living units.

Gross Income Multiplier (GIM)

A **GIM** is *a factor that takes into account income derived from all sources of a property*. It is most often used when there are income-producing capabilities of a property other than rent derived from living units.

For Example
A small residential income property with four units might have garage or parking spaces that rent to parties other than the occupants of the living units. Or, there might be a coin-operated laundry facility on the premises that derives income.

The use of a GIM is appropriate when the subject property produces income in addition to rent from the living unit(s). With a GIM, both the rent and the other income are used for the analysis, while the GRM considers only rent.

There are some special things to know about using the GIM in a market value assignment:

- Other sources of income must be determined legally permissible and to reasonably have the potential to be ongoing.
- The rent and income derived from comparable data and applied to the subject property is considered on an annual basis.
- The income used in determining a GIM could be the potential gross income (PGI), or the effective gross income (EGI) and must be derived and applied consistently.
- The GIM is derived from properties with similar rent and (other) income flows.

The particular feature or additional use of the property for which other income is being considered must be legally permissible by private and public regulations. In addition, the appraiser must determine that the source of the income could be reasonably determined to be applicable and desirable to those who comprise the market for such property.

It is most common for GIMs to be derived from and applied to annual income. The basis of income derived from, and applied to, the development of the GIM technique could be based on either potential gross income (PGI) or effective gross income (EGI). In such cases, the multiplier resulting would be either a potential gross income multiplier, or PGIM, or an effective gross income multiplier, or EGIM.

Potential Gross Income Multiplier (PGIM)

The **PGIM** is *derived from, and applied to, the total gross income generated by the property without vacancy being considered*. This is probably the most common application of a GIM, and is appropriate when the source of the additional income is not influenced by the occupancy of the living unit(s).

A rather large older residential dwelling in an established neighborhood features a four-stall garage, with each stall divided by an interior wall, which is situated at the rear of the property, along an alley. Two of the garage stalls are for the use of the renter of the dwelling and are included in its rent, while the other two have been rented for many years to other parties for storage. The two rented garage stalls generate $75 of income per month each.

This example illustrates a circumstance when the PGIM would be perfectly logical, since the rental income of the garages is not influenced by the occupancy of the rental dwelling.

Deriving a PGIM from Market Data

The subject of an appraisal, a leased residence generating $7,200 in market rent annually, has a small additional storage building that produces a consistent income of $1,200 per year, based on an annual lease to another party. No similar data featuring a storage building can be located by the appraiser.

The appraiser has located a similar rented residence generating $6,300 in market rent that has a billboard facing a highway at the rear of the property. The space on which the billboard is placed is leased, on an annual basis, to the advertising company for $1,200 per year. The property sold four months ago in similar market conditions for $179,000.

While the source of the income is not consistent, the income and the consistent basis from which it is derived are the same. Most likely this is what the typical investor would consider in forming his conclusions about the anticipatory benefit of the investment— consistent like dollars for consistent like dollars. Therefore, the GIM (in this case PGIM) could be derived from the property with the billboard and applied to the property with the storage building.

The PGIM is extracted from the sale data using VIM, producing the following conclusion:

$$\$179,000 \div \$7,500\ (\$6,300 + \$1,200) = 23.87$$

Applying the PGIM

In the previous example, the subject property was a single-family dwelling generating $7,200 annually in market rent. A storage building on the property produced $1,200 per year in other income. The indicated PGIM derived from comparable market data was 23.87.

To develop an indication of the subject's value, the subject's determined PGI is multiplied by the PGIM:

$$\$8,400\ (\$7,200 + \$1,200)\ x\ 23.87 = \$200,508$$

The appraiser would probably round the indication to $200,000, or maybe $201,000.

Effective Gross Income Multiplier (EGIM)

An **EGIM** is *derived using EGI—the amount after estimated vacancy and any collection loss have been deducted from PGI.* The EGIM is warranted when living unit occupancy is related to the potential for income from other sources.

A four-unit apartment building has a small common laundry room with coin-operated washers, dryers, and vending services for the tenants' use. There are no provisions in the apartment units for washer/dryer hook-up by the lessee. At full occupancy, the laundry facility generates approximately $1,200 annually in additional income for the lessor.

In this example, the additional income is dependent on the occupancy level of the apartment building. The higher the vacancy, the less the laundry is used and, thus, income is diminished. Therefore, the income used in the GIM analysis might be best considered from the standpoint of EGI, using an EGIM.

Deriving an EGIM from Market Data

The subject property is a four-unit apartment building with a coin-operated laundry facility. PGI of the rental units totals $2,000 per month. At full occupancy, the laundry facility averages $100 per month.

A recently transacted comparable property has been found within the subject's market. It is a four-unit property with PGI of $1,800 per month, and four parking spaces that rent separately (and only) to the tenants for $25 per month each. The property indicated a vacancy rate of 4.8%, which was deemed to be consistent with the market. The transaction price of the property was $338,000.

While the sources of income are different in the example, both sources of income are controlled by the tenants and influenced by occupancy. Thus, it is appropriate to derive the GIM (in this case EGIM) from the recently transacted property.

The steps for deriving an EGIM are as follows:

Step 1: Determine annual income from rent.

$1,800 monthly from rental units x 12 months= $21,600 annual income from rent

Step 2: Determine annual income from parking spaces.

4 parking spaces @ $25 per month= $100 monthly x 12 months = $1,200 annual income

Step 3: Determine total PGI for the property.

$21,600 + $1,200 = $22,800

Step 4: Determine loss due to vacancy by applying the market vacancy rate to PGI.

$22,800 x 4.8% (0.048) = $1,094.40

Step 5: Determine EGI by subtracting vacancy loss from PGI

$22,800 - $1,094.40 = $21,705.60

Step 6: Use VIM to derive the EGIM.

$338,000 (Transaction Price) ÷ $21,705.60 (EGI) = 15.57 EGIM (rounded)

Applying the EGIM

In the previous example, the subject was a four-unit apartment building, generating $2,000 monthly market rent from the living units and $100 per month from the coin-operated laundry when the living units are at full occupancy. The market extracted vacancy rate given in the example was 4.8% and the indicated EGIM derived from comparable data was 15.57.

To develop an indication of value for the subject, PGI for the subject must first be calculated:

$24,000	**($2,000 rent x 12 months)**
+ 1,200	**($100 laundry income x 12 months)**
$25,200	**PGI**

Now the vacancy factor must be calculated and subtracted from PGI to result in EGI:

$25,200 x 4.8% (0.048) = $1,209.60 Vacancy

$25,200 - $1,209.60 = $23,990.40 EGI

As a final step, the subject's EGI is multiplied by the EGIM to indicate a value conclusion:

$23,990.40 x 15.57 = $373,530.53

Depending on the assignment, the appraiser would probably round the developed value indication to $374,000, or maybe even $375,000, in reconciling the conclusions of the income approach.

Apply Your Knowledge 3.1: Multiplier Extraction Case Study

A comparable sale is an income-producing property that has 10 units. Each unit has a gross monthly rent of $700. Annual other income received from the resale of utilities amounts to $3,000. The financial vacancy and credit loss totals $3,360. The sale price of the comparable is $380,000.

Begin the first part of multiplier extraction by processing the gross income into:

1. Gross Monthly Rent $_____
2. Annualized Gross Rent $_____
3. Potential Gross Income $_____
4. Effective Gross Income $_____

Multiplier Extraction

Sale Price ÷ Gross Income = Multiplier

- Sale Price ÷ Gross Monthly Rent = **GRM**

- Sale Price ÷ PGI (Sum of Annual Rent + Other Income) = **PGIM**

- Sale Price ÷ EGI (Sum of Annual Rent + Other Income - V & C Loss) = **EGIM**

Use the information provided in the Multiplier Extraction Case Study above to find the multipliers. (Round to the nearest two decimal places.)

1. GRM (Monthly)_____
2. PGIM   _____
3. EGIM   _____

Chapter Summary

1. Multiplier capitalization has a broad appeal due to its simple formula.

2. Regardless of which multiplier offers the more credible indicator, the formula for application of the multiplier methodology is the same: Value = Income x Multiplier.

3. In most residential valuation, the Income Approach is based on the gross rent multiplier, a factor derived by dividing the sale price (value) by its gross rent (income).

4. Market rent and sale price must be scrutinized when being processed to be sure no inflationary item has skewed either component.

5. Documentation of how the market rent and the GRM was derived is critical to the ethical requisite of giving evidence to the analysis that took place while performing the Income Approach.

6. Sometimes the market is not sufficient in quantity of data, which will require qualitative judgment. That qualitative judgment is not sufficiently supported by a statement such as "based on the appraiser's knowledge of the market and years of practice." There must be evidence in the workfile that an analysis has been completed including the sources of information from named individuals.

Chapter Quiz

1. **What is the value of a duplex that has a gross monthly rent of $700 per unit, a 5% vacancy, and a monthly GRM of 115?**

   A. $122,592
   B. $132,400
   C. $161,000
   D. $231,104

2. **Other income is NOT part of the**

   A. GRM.
   B. multiplier capitalization.
   C. NOI.
   D. VIM.

3. **The effective gross income of a property is based on $800 per month per unit in a four-plex. The property has an annualized vacancy and credit loss of 4% and generates $3,600 annually in other income. What is the EGIM based on a pending sale of $450,000?**

   A. 11.16
   B. 15.54
   C. 16.09
   D. 19.17

4. **Often, the availability of rental comparables will exist, but the more difficult evidence is the**

   A. availability of expenses connected with the property type.
   B. availability of sales with tenant occupancy.
   C. information about the subject's rent.
   D. insurance expense.

5. **If a duplex has suffered external obsolescence from a nearby employment center shutting down, what is the impact given gross monthly rent was reduced from $650 to $575 and the monthly GRM is 165?**

   A. $2,900
   B. $8,260
   C. $24,750
   D. $40,359

6. **Which multiplier is based on vacancy and other income when gross income is being calculated?**

   A. EGIM
   B. DCF
   C. GRM
   D. PGIM

7. **What must be affirmed in order for a credible multiplier to be extracted?**

   A. all competing sales must be within two miles
   B. a minimum two-year lease
   C. sales used must have tenant occupancy at time of sale
   D. similar land-to-building ratios to ensure multiplier extraction is representative of a similar relationship

8. **When developing a multiplier, under a market value definition, what must the appraiser do?**

   A. Contract rent must be utilized to ensure the value meets the desires of the investor.
   B. Expenses associated with the mortgage must be factored into the credit loss.
   C. Market rent and sale price must be scrutinized to ensure no inflationary item has skewed either component.
   D. Vacancy must be held steady at 5% to be sure there is consistency in extracting the PGIM.

9. **What is the value of an income-producing duplex if the gross monthly rent total of the property is $2,100 and the monthly GRM is 125?**

   A. $62,590
   B. $125,650
   C. $262,500
   D. $325,600

10. **If vacancy is steady at 4% and credit loss is 1.5%, what is value of a three-unit residential property where each unit generates $10,000 annual rent and the PGIM is 25?**

    A. $535,000
    B. $615,400
    C. $737,100
    D. $750,000

Chapter 4:

Expenses of an Income Stream

Chapter Objectives

After completing this chapter, you will be able to:

- Define the process of formulating the estimate of a future dollar amount needed.
- Identify how to calculate the annual payment future worth at a compounded rate of interest.
- Describe how to differentiate between fixed and variable operating expenses.
- Identify a reserve estimate for the replacement of short-lived items both straight-line and sinking fund.

Fixed Operating Expenses A set amount charged to the property for the fiscal year, regardless of the income production, whether due to the condition being physical or economic.

FW1 Future worth of $1.

Mill Based upon a Latin word that means "thousandth". A mill is 1/1000th of a dollar, or $0.001.

Mill rate The number of mills per dollar of the tax-assessed value.

Reserves Expenses that represent monies or costs held for future replacements.

Reserves for Replacement An amount withheld over and above expenses of day-to-day operation for replacement of short-lived items.

Reserve Study An analysis of what will need to be replaced over the investor's anticipated holding term.

Sinking Fund Factor (SFF) Measures the amount of monies that need to be deposited each year into a compound-interest account in order to have sufficient funds for the replacement of short-lived components.

Variable Operating Expenses A fluctuating expense annualized.

Chapter Introduction

Net Operating Income (NOI) is the required development in valuing income property types, such as the detached single-family, small income properties (such as two (2) to four (4) units), or apartment complexes. In the previous chapters, gross income was introduced. This chapter brings the gross income down into the bottom line, NOI. A discussion of what those expenses are, what they are not, and how they are to be calculated is the focus. This chapter also introduces two (2) of the six (6) compound-interest factors when the focus is on the projection of time and how that factor can affect the current NOI.

In every location, there will be, on any given effective date, a surrounding land use and defined economic conditions that will effect (and affect) demand for a specific property type. The demand for the property will affect the rent schedule and its vacancy. The quantity, quality, and durability of the income and its management will affect the credit loss. The surrounding property types competing with their amenities directly impacts the production of other income. Accounting for those market factors (as discussed in the previous chapter) results in the effective gross income.

Effective gross income (EGI) is *the true income reasonably expected to be received before the bills or costs of operating and maintaining the investment are deducted.* Expenses subtracted from the EGI must be those *solely associative* with the real estate. In the valuation of income property, there can be no deduction associated with the business conducted on the site, for the expenses of the employees, or for maintenance of any personal property. In order to process income from an *effective gross income* to a *net operating income*, there are **three (3) categories of expenses** that must be identified, analyzed, and applied to the EGI. Those three (3) categories of expenses are:

1. **Fixed Operating Expenses**
2. **Variable Operating Expenses**
3. **Reserves for Replacements**

This chapter will discuss each expenditure as it relates to the development of a Net Operating Income.

Fixed Operating Expenses

The term "fixed operating expense," in the context of NOI, sets forth to account for those expenditures that are required to be paid annually. The fixed operating expense is *not* a fluctuating cost. It is also *not* influenced by the vacancy or credit loss. A **fixed operating expense** is *a set amount charged to the property for the fiscal year, regardless of the income production.*

Types of Fixed Operating Expenses

1. **Real Estate Property Taxes**

   Real estate property taxes should be viewed closely to ensure the cost is *equitable* and *reasonable* for the market. The valuation of new construction or a new community will require an estimate made under a **hypothetical condition** (*that which is known not to be true, yet necessary to assume in order to continue the assignment*).

   √ **Note:** An assumption may be necessary by the assignment when an appraised value is requested on a condition that does not exist. One example of this is valuing a property as if it were built on the effective date of the appraisal when it is still in the planning stages. For more information, refer to the definition section of the current Uniform Standards of Professional Appraisal Practice (USPAP) published by The Appraisal Foundation (TAF) available at www.appraisalfoundation.org.

Taxes are most often based on a percent of the market value. This is known as the *tax assessed value*. The tax rate is the measure placed against the tax assessed value and can be chargeable in advance or in arrears. Identifying this charge is *critical* to income projections, especially when the forecasted resale of the property is required.

Typically, the tax rate is expressed in a measure known as mills. A **mill** is *1/1000th of a dollar*, or *$0.001*. The **tax rate** or **mill rate** is *the number of mills per dollar of the tax-assessed value*.

Example

The following example will reveal how to use the information provided to find the tax rate charge and assess the real estate taxes due for a property.

- The property had a market value of **$103,000.00**
- The tax assessment for the tax jurisdiction is based on **50%** of the current market value.
- The mill rate for the assessment in the tax jurisdiction is **75 mills**.

Step 1: Find the tax rate charge

	75	(Mills)
X	0.001	(Rate of Each Mill)
=	**0.075**	**(Tax Rate Charge)**

Step 2: Find the real estate taxes due

	$103,000.00	(Current Market Value)
X	50%	(Tax Assessment)
=	$51,500.00	(Assessed Value)
X	0.075	(Tax Rate Charge)
=	**$3,862.50**	**(Real Estate Taxes Due)**

2. **Real Property Insurance**

   Real Property insurance does not include coverage for personal property owned by the tenant or employee benefits. The type of coverage determines this cost. It needs to be clear in the development of this charge to the property's income that the expense *does not* include any other type of insurance coverage.

3. **Mandatory Association Fees**

   Some property types, such as condominiums, charge fees to cover common areas and maintenance costs. There is a set fee annually for that shared service and/or amenity. In some markets, there is a security maintenance fee shared by commercial ventures.

Variable Operating Expense

The term **variable operating** defines *the fluctuation of costs throughout the fiscal year in operating and maintaining the property*. The expense itself reports a sum for the fiscal year. The sum total amount represents those monies spent over a year's period. It is here where the appraiser is most vulnerable in developing this expenditure cost.

Many property owners will have used the monies from the real estate rental income for their personal or other business. In many cases, investors will deduct an amount for depreciation of the asset. This type of book depreciation *cannot* be considered in this expenditure. The types of variable operating expenses will vary with different property types and with lease terms of responsible parties. Regardless of the variance of expenses, it is a cost charged to the income stream to ensure that the cash flow will not be interrupted.

Types of Variable Operating Expenses

Not all of the types of variable operating expenses will be incurred by the income property. It will depend on the *type* of income property. For example, a four-plex (four-unit complex) would not typically have a pool expense, whereas an apartment complex may have such an expenditure.

√ **Note:** The various types of variable operating expenses are cited in this section to increase familiarity with the type of expense that would be expected in order to maintain the occupancy and income production.

- **Management Fees**

  Fees structured around the occupancy of the property and not the potential income are management costs. Professional management fees usually structure their cost as a higher percentage of the initial lease payment and a maintenance percentage charge to the property for the remaining lease period. The duties of the property management can be on or off site or a combination of both. The greater amount of tasks taken on by the property managers will result in a higher fee charged for the service. In general, good professional property management is conducive to a durable healthy income stream. Tenants favor property types where problems are resolved quickly. When management fees are expressed as a percent, the fee is based on a percentage of effective gross income (after vacancy has been accounted for), as property managers are not typically paid an incentive on unrented units.

- **Utilities**

  These charges will *always* exist, even when the leasable units have separate meters. At some point, there will be a cost associated with cleaning and showing the property. The need for utilities, although minimal when tenants have separate meters, will have some cost to the property owner. Additional areas of utility costs can include outdoor security lighting, gated entry operation, and lighting for common recreation areas.

  √ **Note:** Telephone service is a utility charge warranted when there is on-site management involved.

- **Trash Removal**

  Most income properties with more than two units will have a shared dumpster. The cost for the service to remove that trash is a reasonable cost of operation to charge against the income.

- **Employee Payroll**

  Depending on the size of the property, there may be a need to have employees in order to maintain it. Employees hired solely for the upkeep, maintenance, and leasing of the properties may include groundskeepers, janitors, and security guards.

- **Service Contracts**

  Many income properties have amenities that require occasional service. Often, that service is outsourced. This is a lower cost as opposed to paying a full- or even part-time employee. Examples of these contracted services would include elevator maintenance, landscaping maintenance, sprinkler system service, etc.

- **Pool Expenses and Supplies**

  For residential income complexes, a swimming pool is usually expected as a tenant amenity. The cost of maintenance is a charge to the income stream, because the lack of this amenity would affect the occupancy and quality of the income.

- **Pest Control**

  This is an expense falling under the *service contract* expense category. Although often reported separately, it is most often an outsourced cost.

- **Snow Removal**

  In regions of the country where snow impedes ingress and egress as well as common area walkways, there will be a charge for this snow removal, as it is a service necessary to maintain occupancy.

- **Maintenance and Repairs**

  There will always be some type of maintenance and repair needs with any property type. A management that structures periodic checks of equipment will often defray costly repairs that occur due to the lack of a regular maintenance program.

- **Legal Fees**

  All income properties will have their income streams protected by entering into written lease agreements with legal enforceability. Very often, recorded leases have the requirement of recorded fees as part of that constructive notice. In the event of default, certain legal processes are necessary to complete an eviction. All of these legal matters will require the service of attorneys.

   Note: Constructive notice is a legal term that defines a public record notice between the parties—a legal presumption that all parties have knowledge.

- **Redecorating Fees**

  These charges differ from normal housekeeping fees and maintenance fees. Once vacated, a unit will have immediate needs from the normal wear and tear due to tenant occupancy. Redecorating fees can include painting the interior walls, steam cleaning the carpet, replacing broken or damaged blinds, etc. In some cases, a per-unit cost is determined over a specific timeframe, and this charge is placed under the reserves for replacement category. However, the IRS defines these types of costs as *maintenance items* and not *contributions to capital*. Regardless of the category under which placed, this is a cost to any income-producing property.

- **Advertising and/or Marketing**

  Ongoing solicitation is necessary in order to maintain occupancy. This charge is over and above any management charge as it relates to the actual cost for the advertising, such as newspapers, rental periodicals, radio, television, or websites.

- **Supplies**

  The cost for cleaning supplies as well as any office supplies is a normal charge against an income stream to ensure the property is maintained.

- **Bank Charges and Accounting Fees**

  Income streams are business revenues that require documentation and servicing to ensure accurate records are kept for asset analysis of the property owners as well as evidence in returned rental deposits and fees for any non-sufficient funds that may be received. Professional accounting services as well as bank charges for maintaining accounts are part of the operating cost of real estate.

- **Reserves for Replacements**

  This last segmented charge to the income stream is for assurance of capital in the event a short-lived component needs replacement.

> √ **Note:** There are a number of ways replacement reserves may be calculated, with only one of the options presented here.

The inclusion of an item in the reserved contribution to capital is based upon how necessary the item is to maintain occupancy and renew or maintain the economic life of the property. Criteria to establish the need is based on:

1. The appropriateness as a capital replacement vs. an operating expense or capital improvement
2. The necessity and urgency of the need

There are **two (2)** parts of a reserve study:

1. Information on the condition of the property
2. The financial analysis pertinent to the physical condition of the property

The first part of the reserve study, assessment of the physical condition of the property, involves determining the economic life of the component, its current useful or effective age, and the remaining years left whereby the component will still have functional utility. On any given year, this conclusion can change because of both economic and social climates.

The second part, performing the financial analysis, requires measuring the future costs of the component that will need replacing as well as formulating a plan where monies can be deposited as well as withdrawn and still maintain a balance sufficient to continue the operation of the property.

There are two (2) economic thoughts on maintaining this fund, should the fund be maintained to:

1. Keep the fund fully maintained
2. Hold from the income stream an amount to baseline fund the reserve account

The baseline funding is a riskier venture, as it keeps the reserve cash balance above zero, but has little or no margin for error. In the event any budget for the replacement is impacted by economic conditions beyond those that can be identified on the effective date, there may not be sufficient funding to withdraw to replace those items.

Tests for Reserve Fund Suitability

There are some typical components necessary to withhold monies for replacement. There are four (4) simple tests of a component's suitability for the reserve fund:

1. **The first test ensures the component is a common maintenance responsibility.**

2. **The second test verifies the component has a limited life.** If the component has a long or extended life, it will not be necessary to plan for its economic recovery. An example would be the acquisition of a property that just had a roof replaced within the last year. The typical holding term of most income property investments is five to seven years; the life of a roof is generally between 15-25 years. Therefore, the roof would not be considered necessary to include in the replacement reserve fund. (Some methods consider replacement cost of an item even if the life is longer than the anticipated holding period.)

3. **The third test checks the ability to reasonably determine the remaining life of the component.** Uncertainty about a component's lifespan would support an addition of miscellaneous marginal reserves to be held without defining the item for monitoring purposes to ensure funding will suffice the component's replacement. If the remaining life is uncertain, there can be no assurance or measure of sufficient funding.

4. **The fourth test confirms the cost of the component.** If the cost to replace the item is minimal, then the component would fall under the category of variable operating expenditures and **not** the reserve for replacement.

Reserve Account Payments

There are various methods of payment that may be made into a reserve account. There are four (4) common methods used by investors to pay their reserve expenses. These methods include:

1. **Withdrawing periodic amounts and holding them in a fund until the component needs replacement.** This method is the most often used by the appraisers. The use of this method employs either a straight-line or a sinking fund calculation depending most often on the sophistication of the management and the age of the property.

2. **"Hard-hit" out of pocket.** This can be significantly risky because the income profit normally enjoyed or reinvested into an alternative rollover investment is diminished with the high cost of the component.

3. **Procuring a loan.** This is an expensive method because loans include closing costs and interest charges that add to the total cost of the component.

4. **"Hide and watch."** This method is generally an impractical method, reflecting poor management. Deferring the cost of replacement will generally lead to other items becoming worn at a faster pace. For example, if the window pane is cracked and not replaced, the heat or air loss will certainly increase the utility cost. Further, deferred maintenance has a negative influence on the value.

Straight-Line vs Sinking Fund

An appraiser must decide on an approach for creating a reserve account estimate. The reserve expenditures estimated by the appraiser are calculated using one of two methods:

1. **Straight-Line**
2. **Sinking Fund**

The straight-line methodology appears to be the simpler methodology on the surface, but it also has the greater chance for error. On one hand, the assumption of the straight-line method is that monies withheld from the cash flow are not placed into an interest bearing account. This is impractical by most investor thinking. The second deficiency with this methodology is that it fails to address any future cost of the component at the time it needs replacement.

The appropriate use of the straight-line method for reserve funding would be in the case where the economic life of the property was short and the condition of the property was such that a discounting of the income for probable costs of renovation would be a more practical view of the income stream.

Example: Straight-Line Reserve Accounting

The following information describes a subject property in a low-rise residential apartment complex containing ten (10) units.

- Each unit is carpeted (exception the kitchens and bathrooms) and offers separate central air and heating units, built-in range-ovens, dishwashers, garbage disposals, refrigerators, exhaust fans, and dual-functioning bathroom vents and light fixtures.
- The actual age of the building is four (4) years old.
- The holding term is eight (8) years; prices of components are rising at a rate of 1.2% per year, and money-market accounts pay 2.5% for monies held above $1,000 in account.*

√ **Note:** *The rising cost of the replacement and interest-bearing account is **not** a consideration in the straight-line method of calculating the reserve funds.

Reserve for Replacements						
Straight-Line Method						
Based on 8 Year Holding Term-Only components with a remaining life of 8 years or less are funded						
Short-Lived Component	**Per Unit Current Cost New**	**Years of Useful Life**	**Actual Yr.'s Age**	**Remaining Yr.'s Life**	**Number of Components**	**Total Dollars to Withhold**
Roof	$6,700	18	4	14	1	N/A
Dishwasher	$200	10	4	6	10	$333
Range Oven	$390	12	4	8	10	$488
Garbage Disposal	$95	7	4	3	10	$317
Refrigerator	$400	15	4	11	10	N/A
Kitchen Fan Hood	$170	15	4	11	10	N/A
Floor Cover Vinyl Roll Tile	$350	15	4	11	10	N/A
Floor Cover Carpet	$1,200	8	4	4	10	$3,000
Bathroom Fan	$70	12	4	8	10	$88
Electrical	$1,650	18	4	14	10	N/A
Plumbing	$1,800	18	4	14	10	N/A
Heating and Air Condition	$1,250	8	4	4	10	$3,125
Total	**$14,275**					**$7,351**

Comment: Those items having a greater life remaining than the anticipated holding term of more than eight (8) years **are not** considered in the withholding of funds. The reason for that economic analysis decision is that a prudent investor would not withhold from the annual profit monies that could benefit the investor at a higher rate of return in other types of investments.

The straight-line formula for calculating reserves is:

Cost per Unit ÷ Years Remaining x Number of Units = Amount to Withhold

Often the question will arise: "Why is personal property, such as refrigerators and ovens, included in the reserves?" If there is no refrigerator or if the refrigerator stops working, the tenant will not want to occupy the property. In the Income Approach, some personal property will be necessary to consider in the reserve account.

Case Study: Using the Straight-Line Approach

The following information describes a case study involving a subject property. Complete the chart using the straight-line method to calculate the monies needed in the subject's account. Remember, the calculation of the Total Dollars to Withhold is limited to whether or not the component is anticipated to need replacing over the next seven (7) years.

The Subject Property:

- A five (5)-unit complex
- Anticipated holding term of seven (7) years
- The actual age of the property is six (6) years

Reserve Account						
7-Year Holding Term						
Short-Lived Component	**Per Unit Current Cost New**	**Years of Useful Life**	**Actual Age in Years**	**Life Remaining in Years**	**Number of Units**	**Total Dollars to Withhold**
Roof	$4,000	18	6	12	1 Bldg.	
Dishwasher	$200	10	6	4	5	
Range Oven	$350	12	6	6	5	
Garbage Disposal	$100	8	6	2	5	
Refrigerator	$270	15	6	9	5	
Kitchen Fan Hood	$125	15	6	9	5	
Floor Cover Vinyl Roll Tile	$350	15	6	9	5	
Floor Cover Carpet	$1,100	8	6	2	5	
Bathroom Fan	$70	12	6	6	5	
Electrical	$1,650	18	6	12	5	
Plumbing	$1,800	18	6	12	5	
Heat and Air	$1,250	8	6	6	5	
Total						

Sinking Fund Reserve Estimate: Using Compound Interest in Calculating the Reserves

Prudent managers often request a **reserve study** (*an analysis of what will need to be replaced over the investor's anticipated holding term*). The sinking fund method is often used to calculate the amount needed to fund a reserve account because it employs the use of compound interest. **Compound interest** is *a tool used to factor the concept of time and impact on value when time is considered.* Each factor represents **$1**, because it is used as a multiplier depending on whether the quest is to measure the present worth from a future amount or amount needed versus forecasting the future worth of a known current amount.

The **Sinking Fund Factor (SFF)** *measures the amount of monies that need to be deposited each year into a compound-interest account in order to have sufficient funds for the replacement of short-lived components.* The **time factor** is *what will have a probable life's end during the holding term of the investment.* A known future amount needed is required to consider the period of time between the present and future. The conclusion of the SFF is a payment. That payment is the amount that will be withheld and assumed to be deposited in an interest-bearing account to reach the future amount needed. By doing so, the income to withhold is not as severe as the amount calculated using the straight-line method.

Reserves are *expenses that represent monies or costs held for future replacements.* Under that reasoning, the assumption must be that change is *highly probable* during the period of holding the investment. After establishing the physical condition of the component, determining its remaining life, and concluding that it has a high degree of needing replacement during the investment holding term, the appraiser needs a projection of the future cost. Through understanding compound interest, often known as "the six functions of $1," the appraiser can forecast the future cost of the replacement through utilizing the Future Worth of $1 (FW1) factor.

The compound interest factor **FW1** *allows a multiplier to be applied to the current cost new in order to ensure sufficient funds exist when the component needs replacing.*

Example Sinking Fund Reserve Estimates

The following example provides a list of information regarding an improvement for a subject property. Observe the steps taken to find the estimate of what a stove replacement will cost at the end of three years.

The monies for a replacement reserves will be placed in an interest bearing account with an annual compound-interest rate of 2.5%.

- The stove in the unit has a current cost new of **$275**.
- The useful life of a stove is **twelve (12) years**.
- The current age of the stove is **nine (9) years**.
- The stove will need to be replaced in **three (3) years**.
- Inflation for appliances is **1.2% per year**.

Example Sinking Fund Reserve Estimates (cont.)

FW1 Formula:

$(1 + i)^n$

$(1 + \text{inflation percent per year})^{\text{years left before replacement}}$

$(1 + 0.012)^3$

$(1 + 0.012) \times (1 + 0.012) \times (1 + 0.012) =$

$1.012 \times 1.012 \times 1.012 = 1.036434$

FW1 Factor	1.036434
Current Cost	x $275.00
Future Cost	**$ 285.02**

The stove will cost $285.02 at end of three years.

Establishing the future cost of the stove will then employ the SFF to determine the amount necessary to deposit each year in order to have $285.02 in the future.

The calculation could also be developed using a financial calculator, such as the HP-12C. The keystrokes would be:

275 PV; 3 n; 1.2 i; Solve for FV

Sinking Fund Factor Formula:

$$\frac{i}{FW1 - 1.00}$$

The interest account pays **0.025 (2.5%) annually**. For the sinking fund factor to work, the FW1 Factor must first be calculated at the **0.025 rate**.

FW1 Formula:

$(1 + i)^n$

$(1 + 0.025) \times (1 + 0.025) \times (1 + 0.025) =$

1.025 x 1.025 x 1.025 = 1.076891 FW1 Factor

SFF Formula:

$$\frac{i}{FW1 - 1.00}$$

$= 0.025 \div (1.076891 - 1.00)$

$= 0.025 \div 0.076891$

= 0.325136   (Sinking Fund Factor)

X $ 285.02   (Future Cost of Stove in Three Years)

= $ 92.67   (Annual Amount Necessary to Deposit)

The amount necessary to withhold annually from the income stream for the stove that needs replacing in three (3) years is **$92.67**. That amount, when deposited each year for a period of three years, will grow to the future amount needed: **$285.02**.

Example Sinking Fund Reserve Estimates (cont.)

The calculation could also be developed using a financial calculator, such as the HP-12C. The keystrokes would be:

285.02 FV; 3 n; 2.5 i; Solve for PMT

Proving sufficiency of the reserve account is possible with the **FW1/P function**.

FW1/P Formula:

$$\frac{FW1 - 1.00}{i}$$

= $(1.076891 - 1.00) \div 0.025$

= $0.76891 \div 0.025$

= 3.075640 (Future Worth of 1 per period factor)

X $ 92.67 (Amount to be Deposited Each Year for Three (3) Years)

= **$285.02** (Future Value of the Annual Deposits in Reserves for the Replacement of the Stove)

The calculation could also be developed using a financial calculator, such as the **HP-12C**. The keystrokes would be:

92.67 PMT; 3 n; 2.5 i; Solve for FV

In Chapter 7, a more comprehensive study will be devoted to compound interest. What is relevant at this point is to understand that reserves are funds held from the income stream in order to have a sufficiency of monies when items affecting the occupancy need to be replaced.

Case Study: Estimating Reserve Accounts

Using the Future Worth of $1 (FW1) and Sinking Fund Factor (SFF) Chart of Compound Interest, calculate the amount of monies that would need to be held in a reserve account based on the case study below the charts. Report your conclusions in the provided grid.

Sinking Fund Factor Chart	
Annual Compounded 5% Rate	
Year	SFF
1	1.000000
2	0.487805
3	0.317209
4	0.232012
5	0.180975
6	0.147017
7	0.122820
8	0.104722
9	0.090690
10	0.079505

Future Worth of $1 Chart	
Annual Rate of Interest 2%	
Year	FW 1 Factor
1	1.020000
2	1.040400
3	1.061208
4	1.082432
5	1.104081
6	1.126162
7	1.148686
8	1.71659
9	1.195093
10	1.218994

- The five unit complex is **six (6) years actual age**.
- The residential income complex is being purchased with an anticipated holding term of **seven (7) years**.
- The interest-bearing account for the reserve pays an **annual 5%**.
- Inflation for cost of replacement components is **2% per year**.

Case Study: Estimating Reserve Accounts (cont.)

Reserves for Replacements

Use the charts, on previous page, to calculate the estimate for the reserves. You will need to identify the cost new, then multiple the cost new by the FW1 factor for the remaining years under seven (7) in order to estimate the future cost new. Once you have identified the future cost new, apply the SFF for the remaining years. This result is the annual deduction from the income for the replacement of short-lived items.

Reserve for Replacements							
Based on 7-Year Holding							
Short-Lived Component	**Per Unit Current Cost New**	**Years of Useful Life**	**Actual Age**	**Life Remaining**	**Future Cost New**	**Number Units/**	**Total Dollars to Withhold**
Roof	$4,000	18	6	12			
Dishwasher	$200	10	6	4			
Range Oven	$350	12	6	6			
Garbage Disposal	$100	8	6	2			
Refrigerator	$270	15	6	9			
Kitchen Fan Hood	$125	15	6	9			
Floor Cover Vinyl Roll Tile	$350	15	6	9			
Floor Cover Carpet	$1,100	8	6	2			
Bathroom Fan	$70	12	6	6			
Electrical	$1,650	18	6	12			
Plumbing	$1,800	18	6	12			
Heat and Air	$1,250	8	6	2			
Total							

Expenses Not Included in the NOI

The income statement reflects the real estate as the source of income, not the individual owner or investor. If the land and improvements could speak, they would say, "*This is how much I can generate, and these are the expenses necessary to maintain my cash flow.*" The land and improvements do not need to negotiate or be concerned with yields of return.

The Net Operating Income statement is an economic report of what the property can generate in net income on a particular day in a particular location as it is specifically improved.

Further, when studying the relationship of the income to value (the focus of subsequent chapters), the appraiser must understand a market that transacts with debt leveraging has the financing built into the capitalization rate (a factor that converts income into value). To incorporate the debt service in the Net Operating Income statement would burden the income and have a double indemnity effect on the capitalization rate itself.

Financial components found in accounting statements, ***but are not*** part of the NOI statement are:

- Corporate Taxes
- Corporate Director's Fees
- Depreciation
- Franchise Taxes
- Mortgage Amortization
- Mortgage Interest
- Mortgage Life Insurance
- Personal Tax Consequences of the Investor
- Personal Property Loans on Equipment that Generates "Other Income"

Chapter Summary

1. NOI statements require gross income to process for three (3) categories of expenses.

2. Fixed operating expenses are those annual costs regardless of the occupancy.

3. Variable operating expenses fluctuate throughout the year and are impacted to a certain extent by the occupancy.

4. Reserve expenses are monies held from the income stream to have on hand for the replacement of short-lived items that can affect the occupancy if they are not immediately replaced when broken.

5. Compound interest is a factor used in the NOI. It considers the impact of time on the estimate of reserves for replacement.

6. Reserve accounts are typically formulated based on the projected holding term of the investor.

Chapter Quiz

1. **What is the amount to be held in a reserve account for a range/oven having a future cost of $700, when the sinking fund factor for three years at 5% is 0.317209?**
   A. $132.40
   B. $152.92
   C. $222.05
   D. $315.89

2. **Which of the following represents monies withheld over and above expenses of day-to-day operation?**
   A. fixed expenses
   B. NOI expenses
   C. reserves expenses
   D. variable operating expenses

3. **The investor wants to hold the property for five years. The roof is eight years old with a life expectancy of 15 years. The cost of the roof is projected to be $6,500 at the time of replacement. What is the amount that is needed to be held in the reserve account for the roof, using the straight-line method?**
   A. $0
   B. $433.33
   C. $812.50
   D. $1,500

4. **The cost of real estate taxes is up 2% this year. The taxes now due for the property are $15,800. What classification should those expenses be processed under?**
   A. fixed
   B. NOI
   C. short-lived
   D. variable operating

5. **Unit 12 of an apartment complex has recently been renovated and now has all new short-lived items. What expense category will be adjusted to hold less money out as a result of this renovation?**
   A. fixed
   B. future worth
   C. reserves
   D. variable

6. **The utility company just gave a public notice that its rates are going up for landlord-supplied utilities. Which expense category will be impacted?**
   A. fixed
   B. replacements
   C. sinking fund
   D. variable operating

7. **Using the straight-line method for estimating reserves, how much should be held for dishwashers that have a future cost of $420 each and need to be replaced in five years for a duplex?**
   A. $50
   B. $84
   C. $100
   D. $168

8. **Which of the following would NOT be held as an expense to real estate income?**
   A. amortized mortgage
   B. cost to replace carpet
   C. housekeeping
   D. property taxes

9. **What does a compound-interest factor represent?**
   A. the impact of renovation on the current "as is" value
   B. a multiplier of $1.00 at a rate over a specific time
   C. a performance ratio
   D. the principal and interest known as the amortization rate

10. **Net Operating Income is**
   A. always inclusive of depreciation.
   B. always processed for the tax consequences of the investor.
   C. never calculated on an annual basis.
   D. never concerned with mortgage interest.

Chapter 5:
Performance Ratios

5

Chapter Objectives

After completing this chapter, you will be able to:

- Describe how to forecast cost and depreciation.
- Identify how many needed parking spaces should be allotted for proposed or available units.
- Define the process for concluding gross livable area.
- Describe how to calculate necessary equity when debt leveraging is the goal.

Building Efficiency Ratio An indicator of the gross leasable area.

Cost Indexes Indexes used to measure past and anticipated cost new.

Expense Ratio Expressed as a percentage of an Effective Gross Income

Gentrification The displacement of one socioeconomic populous for another.

Index A benchmark measure that has a beginning and end point to measure change.

Infill Development The redevelopment within existing developments.

Land to Building Ratio A measure of the ability to expand a building capability.

Parking Ratio A performance measure that determines the capability of maintaining a quantity of cash flow, based on sufficiency of the parking area.

Key Terms

Chapter Introduction

Value based on the Income Approach isn't simply about finding a conclusion through a formula, such as a divisor or a multiplier. The ability to measure the performance of the income production and its continued durability and quality is found through performance ratios. This chapter does not thoroughly examine all ratios, but it does explore those ratios often used in the purchase and management of residential income-producing properties. Investors use these ratios as indicators of an investment that will sufficiently meet their desired yield as additions to their real estate portfolio.

In mathematical terms, *ratios*, *points*, and *indexes* are used in the analysis of income-producing properties to *convey economic performance to the investors*. These terms are mathematical division problems. They are numerical descriptive relationships of components that communicate a property's operational performance or utility. By understanding the relationship of one to the other, the analyst can form conclusions on the functional utility and economic performance of the property generating the income. The conclusion of the terms is communicated in either *fractional* or *percentage expression*.

The Income Approach and the Residential Appraisal

For the residential appraiser, in good economic times, rarely does the Income Approach become a necessary or applicable part of the appraisal process. As economic downturns cycle in their corrective pattern and the oversupply of housing begins, more and more investors choose to convert their properties into a rental investment. Regardless of whether the property is a detached single-family dwelling, townhouse, condo unit, duplex, or four-unit property, when tenant occupancy increases, the Income Approach becomes a *viable measure of the market value*.

Indexes

An **index** is *a statistical measure of the changes*. The changes can be in stocks, in costs of construction, in rates, or in any number of components of the real estate analysis. The benefit of being able to measure change is the higher degree of accuracy gained when forecasting the productivity of the property.

For real estate investors, property managers, and appraisers, indexes are used when valuing in time increments for retrospective, current, and present value.

- **Investors** are interested in understanding changes over time to better understand the probability of their desired yield.

- **Property managers** utilize the indexes to plan their management of the asset for the investor.

- **Appraisers** use indexes when data is limited in a current market but readily identifiable in the retrospective trends.

In a retrospective value assignment, the indexes for building costs and capitalization rates, are viewed along with the earnings in order to develop both a Cost Approach and an Income Approach. The key to understanding indexes is to understand their role in the measure of time. There *must* be a beginning and end point understood for the time factor and the index measure to be utilized.

Cost Index

Cost indexes are *used to measure past and anticipated cost new*. Just like depreciation is a measure of patterned market reaction, so are the cost new indexes.

Example

If the cost index at the time of construction in 1997 was 325 and the cost to build the office building was $255,000, what is the cost to build that property in 2015 based on a current index of 340?

Measure of Index Change

- 325 index in 1997

- 340 index in 2015

- Rise in building costs = 4.62% (340 – 325 = 15; 15 ÷ 325)

Finding the Amount in Dollars of Building Costs

$255,000	(Cost in 1997)
X 0.0462	(Rise in Building Costs)
$11,781	**(Amount in Dollars of Building Costs)**

Impact of Index Change

$255,000	(Cost in 1997)
+ $11,781	(Amount in Dollars of Building Costs)
$266,781	(Impact of Index Change)

Depreciation Factors and Economic Inflation Measured by Index Changes

If a property type is studied over time, within a certain location, the economic conditions can be analyzed *concurrently* with that property type's change in demand over the life of its investment. The change can be reviewed from both a *cost standpoint* and an *income standpoint*.

Example: Today's Value

Let's say depreciation factors for the example above were shown to be **0.98 for each year of actual life** and land prices were rising at **2% per year**. If the year is 2015, what conclusion could be made about the current value, given an **economic life of 40 years for the property**, when the land was valued in 1997 at **$64,000**?

According to the index change of 4.62% for a period of 18 years, the change in cost new is **+ 0.2567 annually**.

Therefore, the following equations may occur (all calculations are rounded to nearest dollar):

	$266,781	(Today's Current Cost for Building Replacement Building in 2015)
+	12,327	(0.002567 Factor x 18 Years = Forecasted Change)
=	$279,108	
-	49,234.65	(Depreciation [0.0098 x 18 Years from Today = 17.64% x $313,841])
=	$229,873.35	
+	87,040	(Plus Land Value [Land Value in 1997 $64,000 x *1.36 Factor of Time])
=	**$316,913.35**	**(Indicated Value in 18 Years)**

Example: Today's Value (cont.)

√ **Note:** The time factor of 1.36 is based on 2% per year of rising land value.

	0.02	
x	18	years
=	0.36	
+	1.00	(to make percent change into a multiplying factor)
=	1.36	

Performance Ratios in Direct Capitalization

When analyzing income characteristics, there are other ratios of performance to consider. These ratios include:

- Parking Ratios
- Building Efficiency Ratios
- Expense to Income Ratios
- Debt Coverage Ratios

These are factors that should be gathered in the market study of the appraisal problem in order to secure comparative performances of similar property types. It is the comparative performance measures by which the marketability of the subject can be identified. The credibility of the income—its quantity, quality, and durability characteristics—is substantiated by the study of the surrounding market and the performance measures of the income streams in the same market area for the same property type.

Parking Ratio

This performance measure determines the capability of maintaining a quantity of cash flow based on *maximum occupancy utilization of the parking area*. When insufficient parking exists, there will be a higher physical vacancy due to the impaired utility of parking. In commercial ventures, this is especially true when the property is competing with other commercial ventures of retail occupancy. The lack of consumer interest in the retail center due to problematic parking will create *a lack of demand* by the retail tenant whose livelihood depends on high pedestrian traffic.

Example: Parking Ratio Extraction

A building contains 40 units with 120 parking spaces. The parking ratio would be:

$$\frac{120 \text{ Parking Spaces}}{40 \text{ Rental Units}} = 3:1$$

√ **Caution!** If the property was a retail center with a need for high walk-in patronage to support the business, then this parking ratio may prove to be insufficient if the typical ratio for similar retail properties is say 10:1.

Knowledge Check 5.1

Complete the calculations of those spaces where question marks appear.

Item	Comp. 1	Comp. 2	Comp. 3	Comp. 4
Parking Ratio	12.5:1	14:1	28.2:1	?
Number of Parking Spaces	200	140	649	175
Number of Units in the Building	?	?	?	130

Building Efficiency Ratio

The performance measure of the improvement's utility for the property owner is the amount of area on which income can be based. The attraction to the building, once the demand for the location has been met, is the design and functionality of the area to be used by the tenant and its relationship to cost. The relationship of the *gross leasable area (GLA)* to the *gross building area (GBA) is* that measure of the building's performance, expressed as a **building efficiency ratio (BER)**. This is also known simply as "efficiency ratio."

Example: Finding the Building Efficiency Ratio

If the GLA of a building is *5,790 square feet* and the GBA is *6,950 square feet,* then the building efficiency ratio would be:

$$\frac{5{,}790 \text{ sq. ft. leasable area}}{\div 6{,}950 \text{ sq. ft. gross building area}} = 0.83 \text{ Building Efficiency Ratio}$$

Therefore, 5,790 is to 6,950 a ratio of 579:695 or **1:0.83** (reducing to the lowest fraction). This ratio conveys to the interested parties that for each one foot of GBA, **83%** of it is an income producing space. When comparing the subject to other competing properties, a comparison of the GLA and the building efficiency ratio should also be considered.

Apply Your Knowledge 5.2

1. Complete the calculations of those spaces where question marks appear.

Item	Rent Comp. 1	Rent Comp. 2	Rent Comp. 3	Rent Comp. 4
Ground Level Area	3,400	4,500	2,950	4,900
Ground Level Leasable Area	2,950	3,800	2,700	4,500
Second Floor Area	3,400	4,000	2,900	4,700
Second Floor Leasable Area	3,200	3,700	2,600	4,400
Gross Building Area	6,800	?	?	?
Gross Leasable Area	6,150	?	?	?
Building Efficiency Ratio	90.4%	?	?	?

2. Based on the median BER, what is the projected potential scheduled gross rent of the subject if the gross building area is 5,900 square feet and overall rent per gross leasable area is $28 per square foot? _____

Expense Ratio

The measure of net profit before debt service and personal tax consequence is a performance ratio that shows the relationship between the *cost of operation* and the *effective or gross income received*. Generally, that measure results from the comparison between the **expenses** (fixed, variable operating and reserves), and the **Effective Gross Income** (true income prior to the expenses).

National statistics are available on certain property types throughout the county from professional associations. Types of statistical data analyzed and available include:

- Shopping centers
- Office buildings
- Condominiums
- Hotels
- Apartments

These database services report ratios and rents by region. Having this type of information on typical ratios of expense for certain property types provides appraisers, investors, and property managers a targeted break-even point or baseline of operation when data in the specific location may not otherwise be available.

A credibly developed NOI statement requires the analysis of the efficiency in the management and the ability to identify any performance deficiency through the expense ratio. Both the property manager and the appraiser share this analysis and obligation. The appraiser is responsible for researching and commenting on the income's quantity, quality, and durability. This commentary would be impossible without a benchmark for the typical performance of the property type in the market area.

Example: Finding the Expense Ratio

The expense to Effective Gross Income (EGI) in the market area is 22%. Make a judgment as the efficiency of financial viability in the following income expense analysis.

Expenses total $23,000 to the EGI of $58,000. Does the expense ratio present an efficient financial viability and make the subject an attractive investment?

$$\frac{\$23{,}000 \text{ Expenses of Subject Property}}{\$58{,}000 \text{ Effective Gross Income of Subject}} = \textbf{39.7\%}$$

Conclusion of Marketability Impact:

The subject is spending 39.7% of every effective gross dollar received. The market is only spending 22%. The subject will not be an attractive investment in the market unless management can improve the expense ratio.

Apply Your Knowledge 5.3

1. *Extract the expense to EGI ratios of the comparable income properties to fill in the blank (?) spaces in the chart.*

Item	Comparable 1	Comparable 2	Comparable 3
PSGI	$38,000	$57,000	$27,000
Vacancy & Credit Loss	$ 2,052	$ 3,135	$ 1,404
Annual Other Income	$ 2,850	$ 4,500	$ 1,200
EGI	?	?	?
Fixed Expenses	$3,610	$5,016	$2,430
Variable Operating Expenses	$5,820	$9,338	$4,550
Reserves for Replacements	$2,900	$4,200	$2,110
NOI	?	?	?
Total Expenses Fixed, Variable, and Reserves	?	?	?
EGI	?	?	?
Expense to EGI Ratio	?%	?%	?%

2. *Based on the median conclusion, what is the indicated maximum expense to EGI ratio?* _____

Debt Coverage Ratio (DCR)

The DCR is used by lending participants for making lending decisions regarding a property. In the event the debt leverage is too high, the loan may not be approved, even when the credit risk is low due to the property's inability to compete with the risk management of minimum debt-to-income. It isn't a measure of the borrower; it is a measure of the *property's ability to cover in its operation the lien risk of a mortgage.*

Example: Finding the Debt Coverage Ratio

If the NOI of a property is $15,000 and the annual debt service (ADS) is $12,450, what is the debt coverage ratio?

$$\frac{\$15,000 \text{ NOI}}{\$12,450 \text{ ADS}} = \mathbf{1.20}$$

The conclusion of 1.20 debt coverage ratio means that the income generated after expenses and prior to any personal tax consequences of the investor covers the debt service by 120%.

For appraisers, this type of economic information is more readily obtainable from the local lending market. This availability affords a strong support of not only performance, but also *capitalization rate development*.

Knowledge Check 5.4

Using the chart provided, fill in the blanks to find the debt coverage ratios for the three comparable properties.

Item	Comparable 1	Comparable 2	Comparable 3
NOI	$22,755	$36,254	$27,950
ADS	$17,359	$23,640	$18,580
Debt Coverage Ratio	?	?	?

Land-to-Building Ratio

When expansion of income capabilities is being considered, the surrounding land is viewed to aid in the decision. The measure of growth and density of development is communicated in the land-to-building ratio. The term **infill development** is *the redevelopment within existing developments*. Whereas the initial development involved raw land and planning for improvement, infill creates in general *a higher density of land use*. It is the maximizing of land through new land utilization. The risk of infill development can be high without the knowledge and skill of not only the redesign of land use, but also successfully fighting a stigma of a perceived poor location. To be able to attract buyers, there must be a plan that incorporates targeting and procuring a gentrification process of the existing neighborhood.

Gentrification is *the displacement of one socio-economic populous for another*. In many downtown areas, this practice of successful infill development with gentrification goals has been recognized. The once deteriorated residences are now restored dwellings and in many cases professional offices, trendy restaurants, and nightclubs.

Infill development and future-phased development cannot begin until there is an understanding of the land-to-building ratio. This type of ratio describes *the relationship of the land size (expressed in a percentage) to the size of the building or gross leasable area*.

Example: Finding the Land-to-Building Ratio

If a building is measured at 45′ x 35′ and the land is measured 100′ x 200′, then the land-to-building ratio would be:

$$\frac{20,000 \text{ sq. ft. Land}}{1,575 \text{ sq. ft. GLA}} = \textbf{12.7 : 1} \quad \textbf{Land to Building Ratio}$$

Therefore, it can be described that 20,000 is to 1,575, a ratio of **800/63** (reducing to the lowest fraction). This scenario conveys a land to building ratio that results in an area relationship. For every **800** square feet of land, there is **63** square feet of gross leasable area. The ratio of 12.7:1 means for each 12.7 square feet of land area there is one (1) square foot of building. Having this information gives opportunity for considering future expansion.

Loan-to-Value Ratio

Appraisers are required to address financing concessions in their analysis of sales and rental agreements. Loan-to-value ratios are component parts of the analysis of sales concessions and possible financing adjustments. This is due to the closing costs, principal, and interest payments paid on the basis of the loan value. In capitalization rate development, these ratios are necessary to identify because they *represent the loan or mortgage position in the capitalization rate development.*

Example: Finding the Loan-to-Value Ratio

The loan value is $95,000 based on an appraised value of $102,000. Therefore the loan to value ratio is:

$95,000	(Loan Value)
÷ $102,000	(Market Value According to Appraisal)
= **93.14%**	**(Loan-to-Value Ratio)**

Loan-to-Value Ratio Application

A sales price of a subject property is $315,000. Assuming lending institutions require that loans of this level be based on a maximum loan-to-value ratio of 85%, what is the **maximum** loan that can be made on this transaction?

$315,000	(Sale Price)
x 85%	(Mortgage/Loan Percentage Maximum)
=**$267,750**	**(Maximum Loan Allowance)**

Workfile Documentation

For workfile documentation, a form, like the following sample form, is good evidence of an appraiser's data research and analysis of the seller concessions.

Sample Blank Form for Extracting Financing Terms in the Market

Item	Comp. 1	Comp. 2	Comp. 3	Comp. 4
Sale Price				
Loan Value				
Loan-to-Value Ratio				
Interested Party Contributions (Financial)				
% IPCs to Sale Price				

Chapter Summary

1. The analysis of concessions and financing requires the employment of understanding how the loan-to-value process works.

2. The debt coverage ratio draws conclusions of the property's NOI capacity to handle debt service when the property is a mortgage.

3. Prospective costs and depreciation can be forecasted through indexes.

4. The application of a building efficiency ratio affords the analyst the ability to develop a credible rent.

5. Through the analysis of ratios, economic analysts can better form opinions about the durability of the income generated.

6. Conclusion of marketability impact can, in part, be formed based on the understanding of the expense ratio.

Chapter Quiz

1. *A four-plex rents for $750 per unit, per month with a vacancy rate of 4%. Total fixed, variable operating, and reserves expenses total $6,220. What is the expense to Effective Gross Income?*

   A. 12%
   B. 18%
   C. 28%
   D. 35%

2. *Five years ago, the cost index was 350. Currently, the cost index is 382. Has the cost increased or decreased over the past five years?*

   A. decreased
   B. increased
   C. insufficient data
   D. remained unchanged

3. *A parking ratio is 1.5:1. Fifteen parking spaces are proposed for an apartment building. How many apartment units can the building contain and be compliant?*

   A. 10
   B. 12
   C. 23
   D. 30

4. *A sale price for a subject property is $350,000. The lender required a down payment of $87,500. What is the percent of mortgage?*

   A. 25%
   B. 75%
   C. 80%
   D. 100%

5. *The NOI of a tri-plex is $28,000. The property has a mortgage with an annual debt service of $21,500. What is the debt coverage ratio?*

   A. 1.15
   B. 1.22
   C. 1.3
   D. 3.1

6. *An apartment complex is under new management. The range of comparable property expense ratios is 32%-45%. The Effective Gross Income is $30,550. Fixed expenses are $3,800, the variable operating expenses run at $7,200, with reserves held in the amount of $5,500. Is this property operating competitively?*

   A. No, the ratio is 54%
   B. No, the ratio is 65%
   C. Yes, the ratio is 35%
   D. Yes, the ratio is 42%

7. *The gross building area is 5,800 sq. ft. for an apartment complex. The units available for tenant occupancy total 5,510 sq. ft. What is the building efficiency ratio?*

   A. 92%
   B. 95%
   C. 98%
   D. 100%

8. *A subject property's building efficiency ratio is 97%. The GBA contains 6,200 sq. ft. The annual rent is $3.65 per sq. ft. of gross leasable area. What is the gross monthly rent for the subject property?*

   A. $1,829.26
   B. $1,965.21
   C. $2,178.35
   D. $2,312.87

9. *Which is a measure of a property's ability to cover the lien risk of a mortgage in its operation?*

   A. building efficiency ratio
   B. debt coverage ratio
   C. expense ratio
   D. loan-to-value ratio

10. *The formula for debt coverage ratio may be found by*

    A. dividing the NOI by the annual debt service.
    B. multiplying the building percent ratio by the potential gross income.
    C. multiplying the number of available units by the loan ratio.
    D. subtracting the debt service from the NOI and dividing by the equity.

Chapter 6:
Introduction to Capitalization

6

Chapter Objectives

After completing this chapter, you will be able to:

- Define the interplay of the components of a rate.
- Describe how to extract a capitalization rate through the market method.
- Identify how to conclude a value using the IRV method.
- Describe the role of debt leveraging in the development of a cap rate.

Key Terms

Debt Capitalization Rate Known as the amortization factor.

Debt Coverage Ratio A mathematical expression that conveys the relationship of the NOI to the annual debt service.

Direct Capitalization Assumes over the long-term no real change in economic conditions will occur.

Equity Capitalization A result of the return on and of the equity invested.

Equity Dividend Rate The ratio (percentage) relationship of the net profits after debt service divided by the equity.

Financing A means of using debt leveraging.

Yield Capitalization Incorporates the impact of change over a shorter period of holding the investment.

Chapter Overview

The Income Approach, developed on the premise of a long-term holding period, has a very simple formula:

Net Operating Income ÷ Capitalization Rate = Value

The complexity is rooted in the accuracy of the capitalization rate, which is rarely available from the market. When an insufficient amount of data exists, there must be alternative methods for the valuator. The focus of this chapter is in the capitalization rate development for direct capitalization. The introduction to a third compound interest factor, known as the amortization factor, is presented as it pertains to the alternative cap rate methodologies.

Direct capitalization is a method of converting NOI (or I_O) into a value by dividing the NOI by a capitalization rate. It assumes a long-term unchanging economic condition forecast. Another phrase for this process is called *current yield*, when it results in a capitalization rate extracted using the *market method capitalization technique*.

The rate used to convert the income stream is expressed algebraically as $\mathbf{R_O}$, meaning *rate overall*. This rate is also known as an **OAR**, the acronym for *overall rate*. Finally, the rate may also be expressed as the **cap rate**, which is the abbreviated version of *capitalization rate*.

The OAR includes both a return **on** the investment, as well as a return **of** the investment. When land is improved, the improvement is a *wasting asset*. Investors expect to be compensated for wasting assets. To accomplish compensating for the wasting asset, the OAR includes a recapture rate to the investor's risk interest rate (the return on the investment). The total of the two components listed comprises the R_O:

1) Recapture rate
2) Investor's risk rate

Formula for R_O: Market Extracted Method

In a previous chapter, the calculation of multipliers was illustrated with the VIM formula. The illustration presented the formula shown in a triangle where the three components were logically separated to direct whether multiplication or division was required to find the missing third component. You must have two of the three in order to calculate the missing component. In direct capitalization, a similar process is computed with the acronym IRV.

Components of IRV

Letter of Formula	Symbol of Formula	Meaning of Symbol	Formula to Obtain Component
I	I_O	Net Operating Income (NOI)	$R_O \times V_O = I_O$
R	R_O	Rate Overall	$I_O \div V_O = R_O$
V	V_O	Value Overall	$I_O \div R_O = V_O$

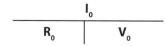

- If you know the income, you will always divide by the other known below the income line.
- If the unknown is the income and the knowns are below the top line, then you multiply R x V.

Knowledge Check 6.1

1. *Looking at the following data, one of the three components in each row is missing. Fill in the blank by using the IRV formula and the complete data of Comparable Sale Number 1 as an example.*

Comparable Sale No.	Comparable NOI	÷	Comparable Sale Price	=	Capitalization Rate
1	$15,000	÷	$150,000	=	0.1000 or 10%
2		÷	$125,000	=	0.0960 or 9.6%
3	$11,000	÷		=	0.1009 or 10.1%
4	$9,700	÷	$95,400	=	
5		÷	$137,000	=	0.0985 or 9.9%
Reconciled R_o					10%

2. *Circle the correct mathematical action for each comparable.*

A. Comparable 1 requires (division or multiplication) to find the missing R_O?

B. Comparable 2 requires (division or multiplication) to find the missing I_O?

C. Comparable 3 requires (division or multiplication) to find the missing V_O?

D. Comparable 4 requires (division or multiplication) to find the missing R_O?

E. Comparable 5 requires (division or multiplication) to find the missing I_O?

Apply Your Knowledge 6.2

Using knowledge gained from the chapters so far, complete the problem below. You will first need to process the income into an NOI and then convert that income into a value.

Case Study	
Potential Scheduled Gross Income	$57,800
Vacancy & Credit Loss 5%	_____
Other Income	$ 3,500
Effective Gross Income	$ _____
Fixed Expenses	$ 4,900
Variable Operating Expense	$ 7,200
Reserves for Replacement	$ 3,200
Net Operating Income	$ _____
Capitalization Rate	10%
Indicated Value Overall	$ _____

Other Methods of Direct Capitalization Rate Development

Although the market extraction method, in theory, is an appropriate method for extracting capitalization rates, it is also problematic. To obtain both sales and quantified qualified NOI Statements that include the reserve for replacements is highly unlikely unless such data comes from previous assignments. Even applying qualified judgments of expenses through published surveys can be difficult if any of the components are in error. In addition to the market extraction method, there are **three (3) other primary methodologies** for capitalization rate development in direct capitalization.

> √ **Note:** *Yield capitalization* incorporates the impact of change over a shorter period of holding the investment. *Direct capitalization* assumes over the long-term no real change in economic conditions will occur.

Other direct capitalization rate methodologies include:

1. **Band of Investment** (Mortgage Equity Technique)
2. **Debt Coverage Ratio Method**

Band of Investment: The Mortgage Equity Technique

Band of investment capitulation rate development involves **two (2) components**:

1. Lender's position and risk for debt leveraging
2. Investor's position and risk based on the equity dividend rate.

The **equity dividend rate** is *the ratio (percentage) relationship of the net profits after debt service divided by the equity.*

Band of Investment Formula:

In this formula, it is important to recognize all factors present.

- **M = Mortgage Position** (The percentage of the L in the LTV ratio.)
- R_M **= Rate of the Mortgage** (The amortization factor, also called the *mortgage constant* or the *debt capitalization rate*.)
- R_E **= Rate of Equity** (Reconciled from comparable sales.)

> √ **Note:** The formula for extracting R_E from comparable sales is: $I_O - (R_M \times V_M) \div V_E$.

- **1-M = Percentage of the Equity Position**

To find the band of investment capitulation rate overall, follow the formula below:

Mortgage Component of the Rate	M x	R_M =	
Plus Equity Component	(1-M) x	R_E =	+_____
		R_O =	

Example: The Mortgage Equity Technique

Financing is available on an 80% ratio. The interest rate charge is 6% over a 15-year term with annual payments. The 6% amortization factor for 15 years is 0.102963. The rate of equity was reconciled at 8.75%. The NOI prior to debt service is $43,000.

(Mortgage Component of the Rate)	$M \times R_M$	$\rightarrow$	0.80	x	0.102963	=	0.0823704
+ (Equity Component)	$1-M) \times R_E$	$\rightarrow$	0.20	x	0.0875	=	0.017500
					R_o		**=0.0998704**

Formula for the Value According to the Income Approach

$43,000	(I_o)
÷ 0.099870	(R_o)
$430,558.73	**(V_o) [Value According to the Income Approach]**

At first glance, this can be overwhelming if you don't possess the understanding of where these different components come from. The lender's position in the mortgage is the loan position. The rate used to measure that component part of the rate is the last column in the compound interest chart, the amortization factor. Let's take a look at each step.

The Rate of the Mortgage in the Band of Investment Method

In Chapter 7, a greater depth about compound interest will be discussed. In the previous chapter, an introduction to Column 1 (FW1) and Column 3 (SFF) was introduced. As previously shown, compound interest is a measure of the impact of time on money. In the rate of the mortgage, it is the factor used to calculate the principal and interest of $1, which is used as a multiplier against the loan amount to compute the principal and interest payment.

In most residential income properties, loans are set up with payments made to the lender (known as the *primary money market*) on a monthly amortization term. **There are six (6) columns in any given compound interest chart.** The amortization column, where the amortization factor is hosted, is Column 6. There is often confusion with this one component because it has so many names/descriptors.

Amortization is also known as the:

- Debt Service Factor
- Debt Capitalizaton Rate
- Amortization Factor
- Rate of the Mortgage
- R_M
- Mortgage Constant

Example: Compound Interest Annual Chart 5%

Year	FW 1	FW 1/P	SFF	PW1	PW 1/P	Amortization
1	1.050000	1.000000	1.000000	0.952381	0.952381	1.050000
2	1.102500	2.050000	0.487805	0.907029	1.859410	0.537805
3	1.157625	3.152500	0.317209	0.863838	2.723248	0.367209
4	1.215506	4.310125	0.232012	0.822702	3.545951	0.282012
5	1.276282	5.525631	0.180975	0.783526	4.329477	0.230975
6	1.340096	6.801913	0.147017	0.746215	5.075692	0.197017
7	1.407100	8.142008	0.122820	0.710681	5.786373	0.172820
8	1.477455	9.549109	0.104722	0.676839	6.463213	0.154722
9	1.551328	11.026564	0.090690	0.644609	7.107822	0.140690
10	1.628895	12.577893	0.079505	0.613913	7.721735	0.129505

Reviewing this annual chart, if a loan of $1 was made for seven (7) years at an APR of 5%, each year the borrower would repay $0.172820 which would total **$1.21**. The bank would be paid back the amount loaned (**$1**) and receive for that service **$0.21** (the interest earned based on the loan made). This is, to the lender, the return "**of**" ($1) and the return "**on**" ($0.21) the investment.

In compound interest, the **Columns 1, 2, and 3** *deal with a future time period*; whereas **Columns 4, 5 and 6** *measure impact of discounting for time from the future to the present*. In this example, if the bank had to wait seven years to receive full payment of the loan, the amortization factor measures the present payment required over that period to repay both interest and the amount borrowed.

The Equity Position of the Cap Rate Using Band of Investment

Most real estate transactions conducted today are financed. **Financing** is *a means of using debt leveraging*. There are **two (2) primary reasons** that investors will use debt leveraging:

1. The investor lacks the cash to purchase the property.

2. The investor seeks to maximize the value of his available equitable cash.

Through debt leveraging, the original investment is the investment with a risk that is commensurate with the money used as a down payment. The **Rate of Equity Formula** is *the calculation of the Equity Dividend Rate*. It is typically calculated based upon the first year's income. That equity will be lost if the loan is not paid in the agreed terms of the mortgage. Because the full amount to acquire the property (such as a cash transaction) is reduced to the amount of the down payment, *the process of measuring the return on the investment* is known as **equity capitalization**.

Just as the lender expects the return on and of his loan amount, the *investor* expects the return on and of her equity. The equity in debt leveraging is reduced because the *equity* has been reduced. To see this clearly, you must first understand how the **equity to income** or **rate of the equity (R_E)** is derived.

Rate of Equity Formula:

$$I_O - \text{Annual Debt Service} \div \text{Equity in Any Given Year} = R_E$$

If the property was obtained as a cash transaction, the equity would be the amount of the sale.

Determining the Rate of Equity

If the sale price of a property was $100,000 (all equity or unlevered purchase) and the first year's net operating income (I_o) was $10,000, then the R_E would be **10%**. That rate is the same rate as the overall rate seen in the IRV, market extraction capitalization formula. The difference between IRV capitalization and equity capitalization when there is no debt service is **not** the method of deriving the rate, but *the focus on the interest*, i.e. the equity interest. Look at the following transaction and note how the equity interest will change once debt leveraging is used to purchase the property.

Review the process of determining through equity capitalization the rate of the equity (R_E) next.

Symbol Legend:

- **LTV** = Loan-to-Value
- **APR** = Annual Percentage Rate of Interest Charged
- **ADS** = Annual Debt Service
- **R_E** = Rate of the Equity or Equity Dividend Rate

Data:

- **Sale Price** = $100,000
- **LTV** = 70/30
- **APR** = 8%
- **Amortized Period** = 20 years, monthly principal and interest payments
- **I_o** = $10,000

Calculations for Equity Dividend Rate with Debt Leveraging

$ 585.51	(Principal and Interest Payment Monthly)
X 12	(Months)
= $7,026.12	**(Annual Debt Service (ADS))**
$10,000.00	(I_o)
- 7,026.12	(ADS)
= $2,973.88	**(Equity Dividend)**
$2,973.88	(Equity Dividend)
÷ $30,000.00	(Equity)
= 0.099129	**(Equity Dividend Rate) or R_E = 9.9%**

When debt leverage is *not utilized,* the return of $10,000 I_o to the $100,000 equity or unlevered purchase price gives a rate of **10%** (i.e., a greater return on the equity).

Financing employs a division of components. There is a *mortgage component* and an *equity component*. The mortgage interest rate seen in the charge to borrow the money is a form of yield rate because it encompasses *time*. The equity dividend rate does **not** consider time in the future or any profit of resale or reversion rights.

The remaining dollars after debt service is known as the **Before - Tax Cash Flow (BTCF)**. When one year is viewed in the BTCF against the equity invested, the rate expressed is the percentage relationship of the cash flow after debt service to the equity.

√ **Note:** In an equity yield rate, the profitability of future events is considered in the rate. The equity dividend rate does not consider any future profitability or loss.

Recapitulation of the Band of Investment

Given there are two (2) positions of investors when debt leveraging is used to acquire property, the *lender* and the *investor*, both positions are factored into the capitalization rate to measure the value of an income-producing property.

Remember the earlier example: The Mortgage Equity Technique

Financing is available on an 80% ratio. The interest rate charge is 6% over a 15-year term with annual payments. The 6% amortization factor for 15 years is 0.102963. The rate of equity was reconciled at 8.75%. The NOI prior to debt service is $43,000.

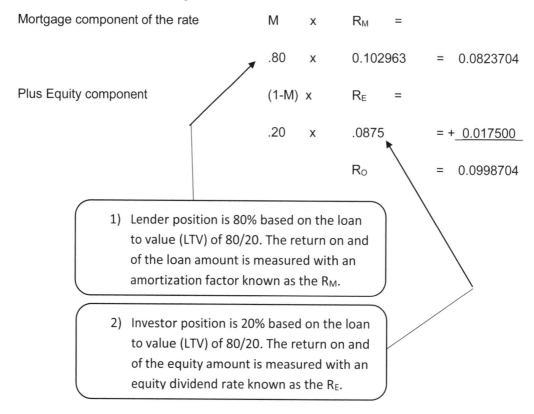

Mortgage component of the rate	M	x	R_M	=	
	.80	x	0.102963	=	0.0823704
Plus Equity component	(1-M)	x	R_E	=	
	.20	x	.0875	= +	0.017500
			R_O	=	0.0998704

1) Lender position is 80% based on the loan to value (LTV) of 80/20. The return on and of the loan amount is measured with an amortization factor known as the R_M.

2) Investor position is 20% based on the loan to value (LTV) of 80/20. The return on and of the equity amount is measured with an equity dividend rate known as the R_E.

	$43,000	(I_O)
÷	0.0998704	(R_O)
=	**$430,558**	**(Value According to the Income Approach)**

The NOI (I_O) is divided by the capitalization rate (Rate Overall (R_O)), and concludes a Value Overall (V_O).

Debt Coverage Ratio: The Underwriter's Method

This capitalization rate considers **three (3) components**:

1. The **percentage position** of the mortgage

2. The **amortization factor** (mortgage constant or debt capitalization rate/factor)

3. A **qualifying ratio** known as the debt coverage ratio

The debt coverage ratio is published either weekly or biweekly at local lending institutions. It is obtained through a formula where: $I_O \div I_M = DCR$. This translates into:

Income Overall ÷ Income of the Mortgage/Annual Debt Service = Debt Coverage Ratio.

Formula for DCR:

$$DCR = \frac{NOI}{I_M}$$

Formula for DCR Capitalization Rate Development:

$$R_O = DCR \times R_M \times M$$

DCR Capitalization Rate Development

Financing is available on an 80% ratio. The interest rate charge is 6% over a 15-year term with annual payments. The 6% amortization factor for 15 years is 0.102963. The rate of equity was reconciled at 8.75%. The NOI prior to debt service is $43,000.

R_O	=	DCR	×	R_M	×	M
R_O	=	1.212453	×	0.102963	×	0.80
R_O	=	0.0998701				

	$43,000	(I_O)
÷	0.0998701	(R_O)
=	**$430,559.29**	**(V_O) (Value according to the Income Approach)**

Chapter Summary

1. There are two (2) primary reasons why investors will use debt leveraging:

   • The investor lacks the cash to purchase the property.

   • The investor seeks to maximize the value of his available equity cash. (This is true if there is positive leverage, either on a yield or dividend basis.)

2. When the total amount to acquire the property (such as a cash transaction) is reduced to the amount of the down payment, the process of measuring the return on the investment is known as equity capitalization.

3. Converting NOI (or I_O) into a value is computed by dividing the NOI into a capitalization rate, and this method is referred to as direct capitalization.

4. Direct capitalization assumes a long-term, unchanging economic condition forecast.

5. When data is lacking to employ the market extraction method for derivation of an overall capitalization rate, alternative methods for which to develop a cap rate are the Band of Investment Method and the Debt Coverage Ratio Method.

6. The mortgage constant is the return "on" and "of" the loan principal, including interest.

Chapter Quiz

1. *The NOI is $31,000. The loan-to-value ratio is 70/30, with the annual debt service totaling $20,483.26. The equity is $93,000. What is the equity dividend?*

   A. $9,239.82

   B. $10,516.74

   C. $62,000.87

   D. $73,483.26

2. *What is the value of a property that generates $18,500 and has a capitalization rate of 9.45%?*

   A. $195,767.20

   B. $219,789.35

   C. $482,450.13

   D. Insufficient data

3. *If the capitalization rate and the sale price are known, what formula would produce an indicator of the NOI?*

   A. Rate ÷ Value = Income

   B. Rate x Value = Income

   C. Value – Rate = Income

   D. Value + Rate = Income

4. *The NOI is $45,000. The annual debt service is $32,000. The equity is $135,000. What is the equity dividend rate?*

   A. 2.5%

   B. 8.7%

   C. 9.6%

   D. 10.0%

5. *The NOI of a tri-plex is $38,000. The property has a mortgage with an annual debt service of $34,500. What is the debt coverage ratio?*

   A. 1.10

   B. 1.4

   C. 2.1

   D. 2.12

6. *Direct capitalization is a one-year point of view of the relationship of*

   A. depreciation and inflation.

   B. land and building value.

   C. sales price and income.

   D. variable factors and risk.

7. *On a sale price of $200,000, what is the mortgage amount if the LTV is 80/20?*

   A. $40,000

   B. $116,000

   C. $160,000

   D. $192,000

8. *The NOI of a subject property is $29,000 before debt service. The pending sale price is $305,000. What is the indicated capitalization rate?*

   A. 5.9%

   B. 9.5%

   C. 10.3

   D. 12.2%

9. *If the annual debt service is $15,000 and the mortgage loan amount is $97,000, what is the mortgage constant?*

   A. 7.2%

   B. 9.5%

   C. 10.2%

   D. 15.5%

10. *What is the value of a property that has a capitalization rate of 9.5% and an NOI of $42,400?*

    A. $95,900.68

    B. $234,789.21

    C. $324,598.35

    D. $446,315.79

Chapter 7:

Compound Interest and the Net Operating Income

Chapter Objectives

After completing this chapter, you will be able to:

- Define the comparisons between simple and compound interest.

- Describe how to forecast future cost based on a compounded rate.

- Identify which column of compound interest is applicable to developing the Income Approach.

- Describe the impact of time on money.

Amortization The repayment of $1 and interest charged.

Compound Interest A method of considering the impact of time on value.

FW1 Future worth of $1.

FW1/p Future worth of $1 periodically (a level stream of payments).

Simple Interest A loan term that divides interest into equal payments.

Sinking Fund Factor A factor that measures the amount of payment needed to deposit into a compound-interest account in order to grow to a future amount.

PW1 The discounting of a future $1 to the present.

PW 1/p The discounting of future level stream of payments to a present value.

Key Terms

Chapter Overview

Real estate investors purchase income properties based on the anticipation of the return of and on their money invested. There is generally a forecasted or expected time the investment is planned. The principle of change states that *nothing* stays the same. Investors in income-producing properties must consider the factor of time when they acquire properties. Compound interest plays a role in the development of income and the capitalization rate that converts the income into a value. This chapter will provide an introductory level into understanding how compound interest is processed and applied to the Income Approach.

Understanding compound interest assists in answering the question, "**What is the benefit of borrowing as opposed to paying cash?**" The benefit is the *opportunity costs of an investment through debt leveraging.* In strong economies where property values are rising, the "bet" on the borrower's side is that the property will have gained more than the cost of obtaining the investment. The lender's "bet" is that when properly underwritten, a loan that has collateral has still been a gain, given the upfront payments of principal, interest, and the collateral of the loan being recaptured at a forced sale.

Arguments have been made that the concept of time and its impact on money has a foundation often based on incorrect assumptions. Followers of that thinking would argue that assuming value today is a discounted present worth of a future asset presumes no plans for the future. The opposite mindset is that all monies invested today will be held for a predetermined time with an absolute certainty of periodic level rates of interest.

So, what other way is probability to be defined? Probability may also be viewed as value and time are subject to the economic principle of change where the forces that affect value—physical, economic, governmental, and social environments—are always in motion. To stop the clock, one must make certain assumptions in order to perform the analysis of risk and returns on investments. *Compound interest* is a useful technique that incorporates the assumption of change over time when performing an appraisal.

Compound Interest vs. Simple Interest

Compound interest differs from simple interest in *how the interest is applied.* For example, in terms of financing a loan with compound interest, the payments made will be mainly applied to the interest in the early years of the loan. The portion of the payment applied to the principal balance will be minimal over the initial years. This is known as an *amortized loan* at a compounded rate. To **amortize** literally means to "*kill off slowly.*" On the other hand, a simple interest loan will divide the interest to be charged into equal payments over the life of the loan. This is best illustrated when one loan is comparatively viewed from both standpoints.

Simple Interest vs. Compound Interest Comparative Recapitulation

Item	Simple Interest	Compound Interest	Difference
Loan Amount	$50,000	$50,000	*NONE*
Term of Loan	7 years	7 years	*NONE*
Principal & Interest Annual Payment	$11,142.86	$9,603.61	*$1,539.25*
Cumulative Interest Paid over 7 years	$28,000	$17,225.28	*$10,774.72*

Comparative Debt Reduction: Simple Interest vs. Compound Interest Method

Simple Interest				Compound Interest			
Item	Principal	Amt. of Principal Paid	Balance of Principal	Item	Principal	Amt. of Principal Paid	Balance of Principal
Yr. 1	$50,000.00	$7,142.86	$42,857.14	Yr. 1	$50,000.00	$5,603.62	$44,396.38
Yr. 2	$42,857.14	$7,142.86	$35,714.28	Yr. 2	$44,396.38	$6,051.91	$38,344.47
Yr. 3	$35,714.29	$7,142.86	$28,571.42	Yr. 3	$38,344.47	$6,536.06	$31,808.41
Yr 4	$28,571.42	$7,142.86	$21,428.56	Yr. 4	$31,808.41	$7,058.95	$24,749.46
Yr. 5	$21,428.56	$7,142.86	$14,285.70	Yr. 5	$24,749.46	$7,623.66	$17,125.80
Yr 6	$14,285.70	$7,142.86	$ 7,142.84	Yr. 6	$17,125.80	$8,233.56	$ 8,892.24
Yr. 7	$ 7,142.84	$7,142.84	-0-	Yr. 7	$ 8,892.24	$8,892.24	-0-

Compound Interest Chart: The Time It Represents

When reviewing the compound interest chart, note what the numbers represent are often referred to as the *six (6) functions of a $1*. This is a multiplying factor, but because it impacts $1, it gets the name reflects its function. The impact of time on $1 can be seen from the future and present time perspective. In the compound-interest chart below, various symbols represent the time period the $1 is being viewed and calculated.

Symbol	Name of Factor	Math Formula	Meaning of Math Conclusion
FW1	Future Worth of $1	$(1 + i)^n$	The result of a future amount or value of $1 deposited and left in an interest-bearing account.
FW1/P	Future Worth of $1 deposited each period	$\dfrac{FW1 - 1}{\div i}$	The future value of a level series of $1 payments deposited each period over the holding term.
SFF	Sinking Fund Factor	$\dfrac{i}{\div FW1 - 1}$	The amount to be deposited each period during the term in order to achieve a $1 in the future (at the end of the term).
PW1	Present Worth of $1	$\dfrac{1}{\div FW1}$	A discounting factor that measures the present value of $1 received in the future.
PW1/P	Present Worth of $1 per period	$\dfrac{1-PW1}{\div i}$	The present worth of future level streams of deposits. The factor is based on $1 deposits that have been made over a future term.
Amortization	Sometimes called the Debt Factor	$\dfrac{i}{\div 1 - PW1}$	The periodic repayment of both principal and interest charged of $1 borrowed over a period called the *amortization term*.

√ **Note:** Although memorization makes these calculations easier, it is important to note that you are not expected to immediately memorize these formulas. In the world of modern investment analysis, financial calculators are the most frequently used method. The chart is presented so that you understand that behind each factor is a formula.

Examine the 6% Compound Interest Chart listed next, which is based on an annual rate of compound interest. Keep in mind every number represents the impact of time on $1 at a specific compounded rate of interest (6% is the annual rate on this chart). The first three (3) columns are based on future value or the forecasting of what $1 will be. In the case of the Sinking Fund Factor, this chart forecasts what annual payments are needed to reach $1 if the payment is deposited in a compound interest bearing account.

Compound interest problems are solved by multiplying a specific number of dollars by the applicable factor. For instance, referring to the chart below, if $10 were held on deposit for 5 years at 6% interest, the balance in 5 years would be found by multiplying $10 x 1.338226 (the factor for the FW1 Year 5). That balance would be $13.38.

$1.00 Annual Compound Interest Chart: Annual Pay Period at 6% Interest

Year	FW1	FW1/P	SFF	PW1	PW1/P	Amortization
1	1.060000	1.000000	1.000000	0.943396	0.943396	1.060000
2	1.123600	2.060000	0.485437	0.889996	1.833393	0.545437
3	1.191016	3.183600	0.314110	0.839619	2.673012	0.374110
4	1.262477	4.374616	0.228591	0.792094	3.465106	0.288591
5	1.338226	5.637093	0.177396	0.747258	4.212364	0.237396
6	1.418519	6.975319	0.143363	0.704961	4.917324	0.203363
7	1.503630	8.393838	0.119135	0.665057	5.582381	0.179135
8	1.593848	9.897468	0.101036	0.627412	6.209794	0.161036
9	1.689479	11.491316	0.087022	0.591898	6.801692	0.147022
10	1.790848	13.180795	0.075868	0.558395	7.360087	0.135868
11	1.898299	14.971643	0.066793	0.526788	7.886875	0.126793
12	2.012196	16.869941	0.059277	0.496969	8.383844	0.119277
13	2.132928	18.882138	0.052960	0.468839	8.852683	0.112960
14	2.260904	21.015066	0.047585	0.442301	9.294984	0.107585
15	2.396558	23.275970	0.042963	0.417265	9.712249	0.102963
16	2.540352	25.672528	0.038952	0.393646	10.105895	0.098952
17	2.692773	28.212880	0.035445	0.371364	10.477260	0.095445
18	2.854339	30.905653	0.032357	0.350344	10.827603	0.092357
19	3.025600	33.759992	0.029621	0.330513	11.158116	0.089621
20	3.207135	36.785591	0.027185	0.311805	11.469921	0.087185

Columns 1-3 *"FUTURE"*	Columns 4-6 *"PRESENT"*

Knowing which factor to use is based on what you *do know* and what you *want to know*. For example look at just Column 1, the factor of the FW1 (or the future worth of $1). Consider an inflation rate of 6% per year. If prices are rising at a rate of 6%, the future cost new can be calculated to *anticipate* that future cost. If you find Year 10, you will see that a dollar deposited today with no other monies deposited will grow to a future amount of $1.79. Subtract the dollar invested to find the difference, and that $1 earned $0.79. What you know is the present; what you are looking for is the future worth of the present $1.

Time and Rate of Interest Impact on $1: FW1

Working with the compound interest charts provided before the exercise, answer the questions below that focus on the forecasting of $1 utilizing **FW1** factors.

Annual Compound Interest Chart 3%

Year	FW1	FW1/P	SFF	PW1	PW1/P	Amortization
1	1.030000	1.000000	1.000000	0.970874	0.970874	1.030000
2	1.060900	2.030000	0.492611	0.942596	1.913470	0.522611
3	1.092727	3.090900	0.323530	0.915142	2.828611	0.353530
4	1.125509	4.183627	0.239027	0.888487	3.717098	0.269027
5	1.159274	5.309136	0.188355	0.862609	4.579707	0.218355
6	1.194052	6.468410	0.154598	0.837484	5.417191	0.184598
7	1.229874	7.662462	0.130506	0.813092	6.230283	0.160506
8	1.266770	8.892336	0.112456	0.789409	7.019692	0.142456
9	1.304773	10.159106	0.098434	0.766417	7.786109	0.128434
10	1.343916	11.463879	0.087231	0.744094	8.530203	0.117231

Annual Compound Interest Chart 5%

Year	FW1	FW1/P	SFF	PW1	PW1/P	Amortization
1	1.050000	1.000000	1.000000	0.952381	0.952381	1.050000
2	1.102500	2.050000	0.487805	0.907029	1.859410	0.537805
3	1.157625	3.152500	0.317209	0.863838	2.723248	0.367209
4	1.215506	4.310125	0.232012	0.822702	3.545951	0.282012
5	1.276282	5.525631	0.180975	0.783526	4.329477	0.230975
6	1.340096	6.801913	0.147017	0.746215	5.075692	0.197017
7	1.407100	8.142008	0.122820	0.710681	5.786373	0.531083
8	1.477455	9.549109	0.104722	0.676839	6.463213	0.154722
9	1.551328	11.026564	0.090690	0.644609	7.107822	0.140690
10	1.628895	12.577893	0.079505	0.613913	7.721735	0.129505

Apply Your Knowledge 7.1

1. What would $1 be worth if it were deposited today in an interest bearing account that paid 5% over a 10-year term?

2. The roof has a cost new of $4,200. What will the roof cost in four years, if inflation is rising at a compounded rate of 3%?

3. The monies received from an unexpected windfall were $12,000. If that money is deposited in an interest-bearing account at 5%, how much money would be available in seven years?

4. There were two investments being looked at, one at a slightly higher risk than the other. What is the difference in gain between 3% and 5% over six years on a $2,500 deposit?

Time and Rate of Interest Impact on $1: FW1/P

The **FW1/P** (Future Worth of $1 per period) is a *compound interest factor that forecasts the future value of level stream $1 deposits each period of the holding term of the investment.* Whereas in the FW1 only $1 was being deposited, in the FW1/P $1 will be deposited *each year* into a compounded rate of interest account. The FW1/P column may be viewed in the following chart as an excerpt from the Annual Compound Interest Chart: Annual Pay Period at 6% Interest. The full chart may be referenced on page 84.

$1 Annual Compound Interest Chart: Annual Pay Period at 6% Interest: FW1/P Column

Year	FW1/P
1	1.000000
2	2.060000
3	3.183600
4	4.374616
5	5.637093
6	6.975319
7	8.393838
8	9.897468
9	11.491316
10	13.180795
11	14.971643
12	16.869941
13	18.882138
14	21.015066
15	23.275970
16	25.672528
17	28.212880
18	30.905653
19	33.759992
20	36.785591

Apply Your Knowledge 7.2

1. *Using data from the excerpted FW1/P column above, find the difference between $1 deposited each year in an interest-bearing account compounding at a rate of 6% over a five-year period versus continuing the same dollar deposits in the account for eight years?*

Apply Your Knowledge 7.3

Working with the compound-interest charts below, answer the questions that focus on the forecasting of $1 utilizing FW1/P factors.

Annual Compound Interest Chart 3%

Year	FW1	FW1/P	SFF	PW1	PW1/P	Amortization
1	1.030000	1.000000	1.000000	0.970874	0.970874	1.030000
2	1.060900	2.030000	0.492611	0.942596	1.913470	0.522611
3	1.092727	3.090900	0.323530	0.915142	2.828611	0.353530
4	1.125509	4.183627	0.239027	0.888487	3.717098	0.269027
5	1.159274	5.309136	0.188355	0.862609	4.579707	0.218355
6	1.194052	6.468410	0.154598	0.837484	5.417191	0.184598
7	1.229874	7.662462	0.130506	0.813092	6.230283	0.160506
8	1.266770	8.892336	0.112456	0.789409	7.019692	0.142456
9	1.304773	10.159106	0.098434	0.766417	7.786109	0.128434
10	1.343916	11.463879	0.087231	0.744094	8.530203	0.117231

Annual Compound Interest Chart 5%

Year	FW1	FW1/P	SFF	PW1	PW1/P	Amortization
1	1.050000	1.000000	1.000000	0.952381	0.952381	1.050000
2	1.102500	2.050000	0.487805	0.907029	1.859410	0.537805
3	1.157625	3.152500	0.317209	0.863838	2.723248	0.367209
4	1.215506	4.310125	0.232012	0.822702	3.545951	0.282012
5	1.276282	5.525631	0.180975	0.783526	4.329477	0.230975
6	1.340096	6.801913	0.147017	0.746215	5.075692	0.197017
7	1.407100	8.142008	0.122820	0.710681	5.786373	0.531083
8	1.477455	9.549109	0.104722	0.676839	6.463213	0.154722
9	1.551328	11.026564	0.090690	0.644609	7.107822	0.140690
10	1.628895	12.577893	0.079505	0.613913	7.721735	0.129505

1. *What would be the balance, if $1 was deposited annually into an interest-bearing account that paid 5% over a ten-year term?*

_____

2. *Deposits of $1,100 are planned to be annually deposited each year for seven years, at a compounded rate of 3%. How much money will be available in the future?*

_____

3. *What is the difference in gain between 3% and 5% compound interest over four years on a $500 annual deposit?*

_____

Time and Rate of Interest Impact on $1: Sinking Fund Factor

The **Sinking Fund Factor** (SFF) is *used to calculate how much money needs to be held in a reserve account.* It requires first the need to identify the future cost at the time the short-lived item needs to be replaced. Once that is known, then the factor is identified based on the *number of years* and the *compounded rate.* That factor, when multiplied by that future cost, will conclude the annual amount that needs to be held from the income stream and deposited into an interest-bearing account, so that when the time comes for the replacement the money will be available. The SFF column may be viewed in the following chart as an excerpt from the Annual Compound Interest Chart: Annual Pay Period at 6% Interest. The full chart may be referenced on page 84.

$1 Annual Compound Interest Chart: Annual Pay Period at 6% Interest: Sinking Fund Factor

Year	SFF
1	1.000000
2	0.485437
3	0.314110
4	0.228591
5	0.177396
6	0.143363
7	0.119135
8	0.101036
9	0.087022
10	0.075868
11	0.066793
12	0.059277
13	0.052960
14	0.047585
15	0.042963
16	0.038952
17	0.035445
18	0.032357
19	0.029621
20	0.027185

Apply Your Knowledge 7.4

1. *What is the difference between the amount that needs to be deposited each year in an interest-bearing account compounding at a rate of 6% over five years versus eight years if $1 is needed in the future?*

Apply Your Knowledge 7.5

Working with the compound interest charts, answer the questions below that focus on the forecast of necessary payments to reach $1 utilizing SFF factors.

Annual Compound Interest Chart 3%

Year	FW1	FW1/P	SFF	PW1	PW1/P	Amortization
1	1.030000	1.000000	1.000000	0.970874	0.970874	1.030000
2	1.060900	2.030000	0.492611	0.942596	1.913470	0.522611
3	1.092727	3.090900	0.323530	0.915142	2.828611	0.353530
4	1.125509	4.183627	0.239027	0.888487	3.717098	0.269027
5	1.159274	5.309136	0.188355	0.862609	4.579707	0.218355
6	1.194052	6.468410	0.154598	0.837484	5.417191	0.184598
7	1.229874	7.662462	0.130506	0.813092	6.230283	0.160506
8	1.266770	8.892336	0.112456	0.789409	7.019692	0.142456
9	1.304773	10.159106	0.098434	0.766417	7.786109	0.128434
10	1.343916	11.463879	0.087231	0.744094	8.530203	0.117231

Annual Compound Interest Chart 5%

Year	FW1	FW1/P	SFF	PW1	PW1/P	Amortization
1	1.050000	1.000000	1.000000	0.952381	0.952381	1.050000
2	1.102500	2.050000	0.487805	0.907029	1.859410	0.537805
3	1.157625	3.152500	0.317209	0.863838	2.723248	0.367209
4	1.215506	4.310125	0.232012	0.822702	3.545951	0.282012
5	1.276282	5.525631	0.180975	0.783526	4.329477	0.230975
6	1.340096	6.801913	0.147017	0.746215	5.075692	0.197017
7	1.407100	8.142008	0.122820	0.710681	5.786373	0.531083
8	1.477455	9.549109	0.104722	0.676839	6.463213	0.154722
9	1.551328	11.026564	0.090690	0.644609	7.107822	0.140690
10	1.628895	12.577893	0.079505	0.613913	7.721735	0.129505

1. *How much money would need to be deposited annually in an interest-bearing account paying 5% over a ten-year term, in order to reach $1?*

2. *In three years, a couple will have a dependent who will require $4,000 in order to attend a school of fine arts for one year. The cost of moving expenses and a housing deposit will be another $14,000. How much money will need to be deposited in a 5% compounded interest account to reach the amount necessary?*

3. *What is the difference in deposits between 3% and 5% compound interest over nine years, when the goal is to end with a sum of $10,000?*

Time and Rate of Interest Impact on $1: PW1

The **PW1** (Present Worth of $1) is *a compound interest factor that discounts a future $1 deposited into a current value*. The PW1 column may be viewed in the following chart as an excerpt from the Annual Compound Interest Chart: Annual Pay Period at 6% Interest. The full chart may be referenced on page 84.

$1 Annual Compound Interest Chart: Annual Pay Period at 6% Interest: PW1 Column

Year	PW1
1	0.943396
2	0.889996
3	0.839619
4	0.792094
5	0.747258
6	0.704961
7	0.665057
8	0.627412
9	0.591898
10	0.558395
11	0.526788
12	0.496969
13	0.468839
14	0.442301
15	0.417265
16	0.393646
17	0.371364
18	0.350344
19	0.330513
20	0.311805

Apply Your Knowledge 7.6

1. *What is the difference in the current value of $1 to be received over five years versus eight years when the discount rate is compounding at 6%.*

Apply Your Knowledge 7.7

Working with the compound interest charts, answer the questions below that focus on the discounting of $1 in the future utilizing PW1 compound interest factors.

Annual Compound Interest Chart 3%

Year	FW1	FW1/P	SFF	PW1	PW1/P	Amortization
1	1.030000	1.000000	1.000000	0.970874	0.970874	1.030000
2	1.060900	2.030000	0.492611	0.942596	1.913470	0.522611
3	1.092727	3.090900	0.323530	0.915142	2.828611	0.353530
4	1.125509	4.183627	0.239027	0.888487	3.717098	0.269027
5	1.159274	5.309136	0.188355	0.862609	4.579707	0.218355
6	1.194052	6.468410	0.154598	0.837484	5.417191	0.184598
7	1.229874	7.662462	0.130506	0.813092	6.230283	0.160506
8	1.266770	8.892336	0.112456	0.789409	7.019692	0.142456
9	1.304773	10.159106	0.098434	0.766417	7.786109	0.128434
10	1.343916	11.463879	0.087231	0.744094	8.530203	0.117231

Annual Compound Interest Chart 5%

Year	FW1	FW1/P	SFF	PW1	PW1/P	Amortization
1	1.050000	1.000000	1.000000	0.952381	0.952381	1.050000
2	1.102500	2.050000	0.487805	0.907029	1.859410	0.537805
3	1.157625	3.152500	0.317209	0.863838	2.723248	0.367209
4	1.215506	4.310125	0.232012	0.822702	3.545951	0.282012
5	1.276282	5.525631	0.180975	0.783526	4.329477	0.230975
6	1.340096	6.801913	0.147017	0.746215	5.075692	0.197017
7	1.407100	8.142008	0.122820	0.710681	5.786373	0.531083
8	1.477455	9.549109	0.104722	0.676839	6.463213	0.154722
9	1.551328	11.026564	0.090690	0.644609	7.107822	0.140690
10	1.628895	12.577893	0.079505	0.613913	7.721735	0.129505

1. *What would a dollar, anticipated to be received in 10 years, be worth today if the discount rate is 5%?*

2. *The roof in five years will have a future cost new of $4,200. Considering inflation at a compounded rate of 3%, what is the current cost of the roof?*

3. *A small lot is projected to be worth of $12,000 in seven years. What is the current value of the lot at a discount rate of 5%?*

4. *How much more can be paid for a property (which is projected in six years to be worth $75,000) if the discount rate is 3% as opposed to 5%? At which rate would the higher yield be gained?*

Time and Rate of Interest Impact on $1: PW1/P

The **PW1/P** (present worth of $1 per period) is *a compound interest factor that discounts the future value of level stream $1 payments during each period of the future holding term of the investment.* This factor is used most often by appraisers to prove the sufficiency of a reserve for replacement fund. Once the payments are determined, a double-check is performed to be certain those payments that are to be deposited will be a sufficient amount to pay for the short-lived item.

The second reason this PW1/P is useful is to value a lease. When the lease is committed for a certain period of time, those level stream payments can be multiplied by a PW1/P factor to value the current/present worth of the lease. The PW1/P column may be viewed in the excerpt from the Annual Compound Interest Chart: Annual Pay Period at 6% Interest. The full chart may be referenced on page 84.

$1 Annual Compound Interest Chart: Annual Pay Period at 6% Interest: PW1/P Column

Year	PW1/P
1	0.943396
2	1.833393
3	2.673012
4	3.465106
5	4.212364
6	4.917324
7	5.582381
8	6.209794
9	6.801692
10	7.360087
11	7.886875
12	8.383844
13	8.852683
14	9.294984
15	9.712249
16	10.105895
17	10.477260
18	10.827603
19	11.158116
20	11.469921

Apply Your Knowledge 7.8

What is the difference between a series of $1 payments to be received each year in the future when the discount rate is 6% over the next five-year period versus continuing the same $1 deposits discounted over an eight-year period?

Apply Your Knowledge 7.9

Working with the compound interest charts, answer the questions below that focus on the discounting of $1 payments utilizing *PW1/P* factors.

Annual Compound Interest Chart 3%

Year	FW1	FW1/P	SFF	PW1	PW1/P	Amortization
1	1.030000	1.000000	1.000000	0.970874	0.970874	1.030000
2	1.060900	2.030000	0.492611	0.942596	1.913470	0.522611
3	1.092727	3.090900	0.323530	0.915142	2.828611	0.353530
4	1.125509	4.183627	0.239027	0.888487	3.717098	0.269027
5	1.159274	5.309136	0.188355	0.862609	4.579707	0.218355
6	1.194052	6.468410	0.154598	0.837484	5.417191	0.184598
7	1.229874	7.662462	0.130506	0.813092	6.230283	0.160506
8	1.266770	8.892336	0.112456	0.789409	7.019692	0.142456
9	1.304773	10.159106	0.098434	0.766417	7.786109	0.128434
10	1.343916	11.463879	0.087231	0.744094	8.530203	0.117231

Annual Compound Interest Chart 5%

Year	FW1	FW1/P	SFF	PW1	PW1/P	Amortization
1	1.050000	1.000000	1.000000	0.952381	0.952381	1.050000
2	1.102500	2.050000	0.487805	0.907029	1.859410	0.537805
3	1.157625	3.152500	0.317209	0.863838	2.723248	0.367209
4	1.215506	4.310125	0.232012	0.822702	3.545951	0.282012
5	1.276282	5.525631	0.180975	0.783526	4.329477	0.230975
6	1.340096	6.801913	0.147017	0.746215	5.075692	0.197017
7	1.407100	8.142008	0.122820	0.710681	5.786373	0.531083
8	1.477455	9.549109	0.104722	0.676839	6.463213	0.154722
9	1.551328	11.026564	0.090690	0.644609	7.107822	0.140690
10	1.628895	12.577893	0.079505	0.613913	7.721735	0.129505

1. *What would $1, anticipated to be received each year for ten years in the future, be worth today if the discount rate was 5%?*

_____

2. *The lease payable at the end of a term has five remaining years. The annual rent scheduled on the lease is $15,700 per year. What is the value of that lease, if it is based on a discount rate of 3%?*

_____

3. *Land rent has been agreed to be paid at the end of each year in the annual amount of $12,000 over an eight-year period. What is the current value of that lease at a discount rate of 5%?*

_____

Time and Rate of Interest Impact on $1: Amortization

The **amortization function** (amortization of $1) is *a compound-interest factor that calculates the principal and interest payments of $1 borrowed in the present during each payment period of the future amortization term*. Investors and agents are quite familiar with the amortization column. This is the factor that is used to calculate the principal and interest re-payment of the loan.

For the appraiser and property managers, this factor is also key in the computation of capitalization rates. This chart is based on an annual repayment. Most real estate loans are structured on monthly amortization, which would result in a different factor because the debt service is being paid back sooner. The amortization column may be viewed in the following chart as an excerpt from the Annual Compound Interest Chart: Annual Pay Period at 6% Interest. The full chart may be referenced on page 84.

$1 Annual Compound Interest Chart: Annual Pay Period at 6% Interest: Amortization

Year	Amortization
1	1.060000
2	0.545437
3	0.374110
4	0.288591
5	0.237396
6	0.203363
7	0.179135
8	0.161036
9	0.147022
10	0.135868
11	0.126793
12	0.119277
13	0.112960
14	0.107585
15	0.102963
16	0.098952
17	0.095445
18	0.092357
19	0.089621
20	0.087185

Apply Your Knowledge 7.10

1. *What is the difference between principal and interest payments each year on the $1 borrowed, when the loan rate is 6% over a five-year amortization period, versus an eight-year amortization period?*

Apply Your Knowledge 7.11

Working with the financial calculator and compound interest charts, answer the questions below that focus on the amortization of $1 utilizing amortization factors.

Annual Compound Interest Chart 3%

Year	FW1	FW1/P	SFF	PW1	PW1/P	Amortization
1	1.030000	1.000000	1.000000	0.970874	0.970874	1.030000
2	1.060900	2.030000	0.492611	0.942596	1.913470	0.522611
3	1.092727	3.090900	0.323530	0.915142	2.828611	0.353530
4	1.125509	4.183627	0.239027	0.888487	3.717098	0.269027
5	1.159274	5.309136	0.188355	0.862609	4.579707	0.218355
6	1.194052	6.468410	0.154598	0.837484	5.417191	0.184598
7	1.229874	7.662462	0.130506	0.813092	6.230283	0.160506
8	1.266770	8.892336	0.112456	0.789409	7.019692	0.142456
9	1.304773	10.159106	0.098434	0.766417	7.786109	0.128434
10	1.343916	11.463879	0.087231	0.744094	8.530203	0.117231

Annual Compound Interest Chart 5%

Year	FW1	FW1/P	SFF	PW1	PW1/P	Amortization
1	1.050000	1.000000	1.000000	0.952381	0.952381	1.050000
2	1.102500	2.050000	0.487805	0.907029	1.859410	0.537805
3	1.157625	3.152500	0.317209	0.863838	2.723248	0.367209
4	1.215506	4.310125	0.232012	0.822702	3.545951	0.282012
5	1.276282	5.525631	0.180975	0.783526	4.329477	0.230975
6	1.340096	6.801913	0.147017	0.746215	5.075692	0.197017
7	1.407100	8.142008	0.122820	0.710681	5.786373	0.531083
8	1.477455	9.549109	0.104722	0.676839	6.463213	0.154722
9	1.551328	11.026564	0.090690	0.644609	7.107822	0.140690
10	1.628895	12.577893	0.079505	0.613913	7.721735	0.129505

1. *What would the principal and interest payment of $1 borrowed today be, if the amortization term is ten years and the interest rate is 5%?*

_____

2. *An amount to be borrowed is $15,000. What is the loan payment on a loan/ amortization interest rate of 3%, if the loan term is eight years?*

_____

3. *A sale price is $70,000. The owners are willing to finance the property over ten years at an APR of 5%, based on an LTV ratio of 70/30. What would the principal and interest payments be?*

_____

Chapter Summary

1. Compound interest allows the impact of time to be considered in the value.

2. Reserves for replacement will let the compounding rate of interest help pay for the future cost needed to replace short-lived items.

3. All compound interest factors are based on $1.

4. Compound interest factors are based on either forecasting the future or discounting the future into a present.

5. Simple interest loans will have a greater amount of interest paid over the same loan term when compared to compound interest.

Chapter Quiz

Use the 6% annual compound interest chart below to answer the following questions

Year	FW1	FW1/P	SFF	PW1	PW1/P	Amortization
1	1.060000	1.000000	1.000000	0.943396	0.943396	1.060000
2	1.123600	2.080000	0.485437	0.889996	1.833393	0.545437
3	1.191016	3.246400	0.314110	0.839619	2.673012	0.374110
4	1.262477	4.506112	0.228591	0.792094	3.465106	0.288591
5	1.338226	5.866601	0.177396	0.747258	4.212364	0.237396
6	1.418519	7.335929	0.143363	0.704961	4.917324	0.203363
7	1.503630	8.922803	0.119135	0.665057	5.582381	0.179135
8	1.593848	10.636628	0.101036	0.627412	6.209794	0.161036
9	1.689479	12.487558	0.087022	0.591898	6.801692	0.147022
10	1.790848	14.486562	0.075868	0.558395	7.360087	0.135868
11	1.898299	14.971643	0.066793	0.526788	7.886875	0.126793
12	2.012196	16.869941	0.059277	0.496969	8.383844	0.119277
13	2.132928	18.882138	0.052960	0.468839	8.852683	0.112960
14	2.260904	21.015066	0.047585	0.442301	9.294984	0.107585
15	2.396558	23.275970	0.042963	0.417265	9.712249	0.102963
16	2.540352	25.672528	0.038952	0.393646	10.105895	0.098952
17	2.692773	28.212880	0.035445	0.371364	10.477260	0.095445
18	2.854339	30.905653	0.032357	0.350344	10.827603	0.092357
19	3.025600	33.759992	0.029621	0.330513	11.158116	0.089621
20	3.207135	36.785591	0.027185	0.311805	11.469921	0.087185

1. **What is the primary difference between compound and simple interest?**

   A. Compound and simple interests are interchangeable terms. There is no difference.

   B. Compound interest is generally a short-term holding period.

   C. The interest is applied differently in each case.

   D. Payments are higher in a simple interest loan.

2. **If costs are rising at 6% per year, what will the carpet (with a current cost of $3,000) cost in five years?**

   A. $2,450.13

   B. $3,180.45

   C. $4,014.68

   D. $5,789.35

3. **Which compound interest factor is used to estimate annual payments to deposit for the reserves for replacement?**

   A. amortization

   B. FW1/P

   C. PW1

   D. sinking fund factor

4. **In developing a cap rate using the Band of the Investment method, which factor would be used to calculate the lender component known as the R_M?**

   A. amortization

   B. PW1

   C. PW1/P

   D. sinking fund factor

5. **In four years, a property's appliances are estimated to have a future cost of $2,500. If the reserve account is paying 6% at a compounded rate, what annual payments must be deposited to reach that future amount?**

   A. $250.98

   B. $328.34

   C. $571.48

   D. $625.12

6. **To amortize means to**

   A. divide equally.

   B. establish a performance ratio.

   C. kill off slowly.

   D. set aside reserve funding.

7. **If land is currently worth $50,000, what will it be worth at the end of a projected investment holding term for eight years, if prices are rising at a compounded rate of 6%?**

   A. $79,692.40

   B. $82,765.32

   C. $83,456.89

   D. $101,934.78

8. **What factor would be used to discount a lease?**

   A. amortization

   B. FW1/P

   C. PW1/P

   D. sinking fund factor

9. **What is the amount that must be held annually in a reserve account for a roof projected to cost $7,000 in 12 years, based on a 6% compound interest-bearing account?**

   A. $414.94

   B. $583.33

   C. $637.25

   D. $708.28

10. **Compound interest allows the factor of _____ to be considered in the value.**

    A. employment rates

    B. exchange rates

    C. federal taxes

    D. time